FAMILY
SCRAPBOOKS

Miss Hannah 1999

MEMORY
MAKERS®
FAMILY SCRAPBOOKS
Yesterday, Today & Tomorrow

Michele Gerbrandt with Deborah Cannarella

HUGH LAUTER LEVIN ASSOCIATES, INC.
IN ASSOCIATION WITH SATELLITE PRESS

COPYRIGHT © 2001 HUGH LAUTER LEVIN ASSOCIATES, INC.
http://www.HLLA.com
ISBN: 0-88363-935-1

Project Director and Editor: Leslie Conron Carola
Design: Kathleen Herlihy-Paoli, Inkstone Design
Copy Editor: Deborah Teipel Zindell

The page ideas features are from the readers and artists of
Memory Makers scrapbook magazine, published by:
Satellite Press
12365 North Huron, #500
Denver, CO 80234-3438
(800) 366-6465
www.memorymakersmagazine.com

FOR MEMORY MAKERS MAGAZINE:
Creative Director: Ron Gerbrandt
Idea Coordinator: Pennie Stutzman
Craft Director: Pam Klassen
Craft Artist: Erikia Ghumm
Photographer: Ken Trujillo
Contributing Photographer: Brenda Martinez
Photo Stylist: Sylvie Abecassis

This book is co-published by Satellite Press and
Hugh Lauter LevinAssociates, Inc.

CONTENTS

······ ◆ ······

4TH OF JULY

"97"

CREATING A FAMILY SCRAPBOOK

A t first, the task of creating a family scrapbook album may seem a bit overwhelming. There are probably lots of relatives on both sides of your family, some who you yourself don't even know. And there are boxes and boxes of old photos, newspaper clippings, and letters tied in bundles with ribbon, somewhere in your attic. Don't panic. Start small. Begin with the stories of those relatives that you know best. Document the most important events—weddings, anniversaries, birthdays. Then you can expand on any topic or theme that you want—family picnics, the arrival at Ellis Island, opening day of the first family business, long-dreamed-of reunions.

To inspire you, we filled this book with the work of many creative scrapbookers who were inspired to record their family heritage in their own individual ways. And, we also invited colleagues, friends, and family members at Memory Makers to design and create some scrapbook pages—both heritage and contemporary pages—from their own lives, and to work with material contributed by others. In this way we could offer a variety of design possibilities using material from many different sources. You will find pages that are remarkable works of art, complex in scope and presentation—the whole nine yards, as they say— and others that are extremely simple. But all share one element: the pages have been created with a strong sense of the art of presentation.

Some of the scrapbook artists were asked to work with the idea of the family tree—to trace the long family line in a compact and visually appealing way. What a perfect place to start if you're stumped as to how to begin. Find out as much as you can about the relatives that are still living. Tell your aunts, uncles, cousins about your interest in researching the family history. Their stories may surprise you. There are sources at the library and on the Internet to help you research your genealogy. You may also be able to locate a genealogical society in the region where you live. You will want to research your information carefully before recording it, to be sure

◂ 4TH OF JULY, HEATHER MCWHORTER, KOKOMO, INDIANA

An Independence Day celebration is preserved with small star-cropped photos and tiny stars punched from red, blue, and opalescent stickers exploding from festive fireworks.

▸ AUTUMN BEAUTY, KAREN KRONE, FLORISSANT, MISSOURI

Fall photos cut with diamond-shaped templates and arranged into a quilt create a colorful geometric record of a family's visit to Lake of the Ozarks.

that it is accurate. Several software manufacturers have developed computer software that helps you research and record your genealogy on the computer.

FAMILY TREASURES

Sometimes the story begins with an object. Pieces of an old quilt, a Western Union telegram, an ornate silver locket, a lock of hair, a colorful hand-painted trunk. Many of our

▲ SEASONS OF OUR FAMILY, ARTWORK: ERIKIA GHUMM, BRIGHTON, COLORADO, PHOTOS: SHARON DOMINGUEZ, THORNTON, COLORADO

When you research your family tree, start with yourself. A page such as this one with few details allows you to get more creative with the page design, and can prepare you for more extensive family tree pages later on. The photos are simply cropped; the hand-cut leaves supply the journaling platform.

MY GRANDPAS

John Patrick Spear Sr. & J.P.

My Grandpas
and I
We laugh
and play
I'm my
Grandpas' boy
In every
way!

September
7th,
1998

Earl Junior Walker & J.P.

GATHERING INFORMATION FROM FAMILY

Gathering information for your album from older family members can be great fun. We all know that experience is the best teacher, so why not take advantage of the the life experiences of our elders.

• Tape record an interview with your grandparents—hear them talk about their lives in their own words. Have a prepared list of questions for them, but encourage them to add stories as they remember.

• What are their hobbies?

• What are their favorite life moments?

• What were the moments that taught them the most?

• What are the most important life skills?

◄ MY GRANDPAS, KATE SPEAR, CHINO, CALIFORNIA

A simple but special page honoring a newborn boy's two grandfathers. Leaping frogs, baseball bat and ball, a colorful train, and the ultimate toy sports car decorate an all-American-boy page. Double-matted photos on cheerful printed paper in classic red and blue are mounted on a cream background. Names and dates and a short poem are journaled with red ink.

scrapbook artists worked with old photographs, newspaper clippings, and recipe cards as the centerpieces of their pages. Hunt through your own collection of family heirlooms and well-loved objects to see what might inspire you.

Flat objects, like ribbons or buttons, and paper objects, like postcards, photographs, and ticket stubs, can be attached directly onto the page (using acid-free adhesives, of course). Small three-dimensional objects, like jewelry, may also be attached to the pages (using memorabilia boxes or acid-free paper or vellum envelopes). Photograph larger objects—such as furniture, vases, or china, if they are part of your mental image of family—and attach those to your pages. Write about the special meaning of the piece and what you've heard—or still wonder—about it.

Capture the times by putting your ancestors' life stories in the context of the world in which they lived. Consider adding old newspaper clippings of significance, or pages from fashion magazines, or advertisements that tout the newest and latest technology or product. By understanding the everyday events and objects of your ancestors' world, you'll feel closer to them and be better able to relate to them.

Be sure to always use archival materials so as not to damage valuable and precious photographs and heirlooms. With archival papers, inks, and other materials, you will ensure that your family scrapbook will last a long, long time—without suffering deterioration, yellowing, crumbling, or the other effects that scrapbooks suffered in the past.

If you do have any old, crumbling scrapbooks, consider recycling the photographs and stories in them by bringing them to your new scrapbook—giving them a safer and more permanent home.

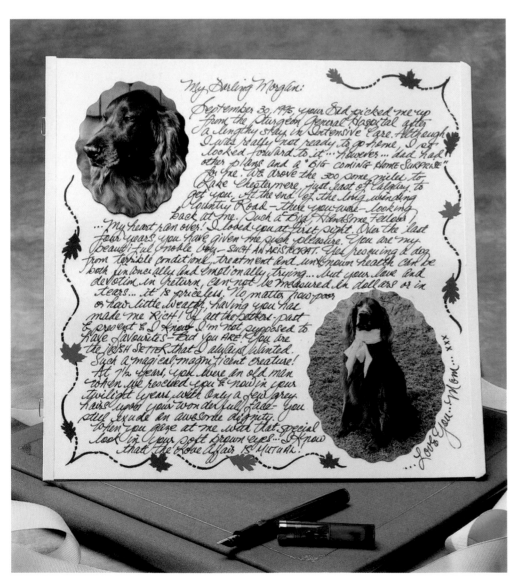

FAMILY STORIES

We asked some of our scrapbookers to focus their pages on a favorite family story, using photos and journaling to tell a colorful tale that may have been told again and again around the dinner table. Your family's special stories will make your scrapbook pages more personal and more engaging than the typical photo albums that simply show one photo after another. Journal to add information, impressions, and feelings, or provide the context of time and event. Be sure to also include stories about special family traditions, funny or surprising anecdotes, special memories, significant historical events, and even day-to-day realities. Interview your elderly relatives, who still remember what life was like in the good old days, or relatives who live at a distance—as they start to talk, they may even surprise themselves as to the long-forgotten stories and details they begin to remember.

JOURNALING

Journaling—providing written information—is an important component of an interesting scrapbook page. There are as many ways to journal as there are to crop your photos. The journaling can be minimal, simple identification, or it can be the main event. That depends on the purpose and style of your pages. The simple handwritten letter of affection for a favorite family member—Morgan, the Irish setter—is one style, direct and clean. You can add color and drama to your heavily journaled pages by emphasizing individual words the way you do in conversation.

▶ MY BIRTHDAY, ARTWORK: PAM KLASSEN, WESTMINSTER, COLORADO, PHOTO: JULIE LABUSZEWSKI, LITTLETON, COLORADO

Tiny illustrations woven into the text, and certain words made bigger and bolder for emphasis are visually commanding.

◀ MY DARLING MORGAN, SANDRA DE ST. CROIX, ST. ALBERT, ALBERTA, CANADA

A long letter from a pet owner to her dog, Morgan, with simple decorations and two photos tell him just how much he is loved. The simple, direct page has a place of honor in a family scrapbook.

◀ REBUS DISNEY SCRAPBOOK, KRISTY HAMILTON, FAIRFAX, VIRGINIA

Rebus journaling is a fun way to present a story and is almost sure to engage young readers—and writers—with the use of small illustrations that substitute for words. These Disney vacation pages literally come alive with the sights of Sea World. Plan your rebus pages carefully so you don't run out of space. Every word—and picture word—is equally important and you want to be sure to have plenty of room to tell your story.

They came by Tall Ship to

The Sydney 2000 Olympics have just finished, and even little Beth, at 2, has learnt to chant 'Aussie Aussie Aussie Oi Oi Oi!' whilst waving our flag. Rory, at 4½, has just worked out that he really is an Australian (he sort of thought he might be Canadian!) So I thought I should take my 'mum duties' a bit more seriously and tell them how they came to be Australian in the first place. So, Rory and Beth... this little story is for you: The first Australians were the aboriginal people. They have lived here almost for ever, but white people like us haven't. Australia is a huge island surrounded by water, and the only way to get here used to be by sailing ship. These pictures are of an old sailing ship called the 'Polly Woodside'. You thought it was a pirate ship because it had lots of piratey things, like big white sails, a crow's nest, rigging, a big wheel to steer with... but no cannons or treasure chests (we looked!). Do you remember how old it seemed? The wind was rustling the sails, and the wooden masts, and sides of the ship creaked all the time. A sailor was climbing the mast and working in the rigging. Seagulls were screeching for food, and waves were swashing against the sides. Beth was really scared of the dark when we went down the ladder, and the cabins where the crew lived were really tiny with little bunks or swinging hammocks to sleep in. There was no electricity, so they were lit by candles. Do you remember the handrail outside the galley (the ship's kitchen) where you thought the pirates hung their towels to dry? Now - close your eyes, and see if you can use your _____ ... _____ ship alive... because ... Once upon a time, a long, long time ago, when pirates really DID exist, people in your own family (who are called your ancestors) sailed on ships a lot like this to come all the way from Britain to Australia. Your first ancestor to come here arrived with the very first fleet, in 1788. Aeroplanes had not even been dreamed of yet, so this was the only way to travel. Ships were pushed along by the wind (motors hadn't been invented), so the trip took many, many months. Can you imagine living on a boat like that, sleeping and eating with more than 100 people in that tiny space, from Easter to Christmas? That was about 240 sleeps! Think of all those people talking and fighting, and being seasick, and the awful smell because they couldn't wash very often except in a bucket of sea water. There were no such things as showers or flush toilets then - yuck! The food was horrible too, because there weren't

▲ TALL SHIP TO AUSTRALIA, HELEN SHIPPERLEE, THORNBURY, VICTORIA, AUSTRALIA

This scrapbook artist accepted the challenge to tell a favorite family story in an extraordinary way. A young mother tells her two young children about an ancestor's hard journey by sea from Ireland to Australia. The sea-blue palette provides the perfect background for the family story written in soft colors against a midnight blue sea. The story is brought up to the present with images of the youngsters touring a tall ship. One can tell a story to a child, but presenting that story with visual excitement is a gift for generations. What a lovely way to remember who you are and where you came from.

a land we call Australia

any refrigerators to keep food fresh, and meat and fruit and vegetables went smelly and rotted, and worms and insects started to live in the bread and biscuits. They must have been very strong people, musn't they, to put up with all that, just to get here? I don't think I could have done it. (And you two can't go 10 minutes in the car without juice and crackers!) Some of your ancestors came because they wanted to - some were soldiers guarding prisoners, some were sailors, some were escaping starvation in the Irish Potato Famine, some hoped to find gold (and did) and some just followed their families. But we have to admit that most of our ancestors were convicts (especially on Poppa's side of the family!) They were sent here as prisoners. They were being punished for stealing horses (and silly enough to advertise it for sale!), lengths of material or receiving stolen goods. Times were very hard then, and most people were very poor. They couldn't afford food or clothes, and sometimes even children were transported just for stealing a loaf of bread. Being sent to Australia was a very, very hard punishment. Most convicts never saw their families again. These first convicts and free people who sailed here were pioneers. There was nothing here to help them, and the first 'cities' were just groups of huts made of sticks and mud, and tents. The settlers had to be very strong and think up clever ideas all the time, just to survive. They built the first houses, the first roads, and the first farms. Everything was strange to them - the hot weather and the funny animals (they had never seen kangaroos before) Poppa's ancestor, George Howell, built the first flour mill, and Pierce Collits went on the first crossing of the Blue Mountains with Blaxland, Lawson and Wentworth. They were both convicts who became very successful free men. The children of these first arrivals, who were born here, were your first real 'Australian' ancestors. Eventually those children grew up and had children, and then THOSE children grew up and had children of their own .. and then, when this had happened 8 times over (which we call 8 generations)... you two finally appeared... and that, my little guys, is how you came to be 'Australian'!

▲ AS FAMILIES GATHER, ARTWORK: ERIKIA GHUMM, BRIGHTON, COLORADO, AND PAM KLASSEN, WESTMINSTER, COLORADO, PHOTO: GERALD TRAFFICANDA

A birthday party California style for Great-Grandma Marie. The simple family photo is treated to two presentations. Both pages are filled with colored and printed papers, stamped and die-cut images, and lots of layers and texture.

DESIGN

When you begin to think about actually putting your project on paper it's time to think about how it will look. What is the purpose of the page? Do you want the photos themselves to tell the story, or is the journaling meant to tell it and the photos serve as illustrations? Both are powerful. How many images do you want to include on the page? Is one more dominant than another? Are you going to mat the photos, frame them, decorate them? What color scheme will work best?

We decided to present two different color treatments for the same scrapbook page to show the effect of color. Look at the two pages above and decide which you like best. Soft, muted violets, greens, and creams are lovely and provide a quiet background for a lively colored photo of a family gathering. A more dramatic palette of contrasting colors makes a strong statement. The bright colors *frame* the central photo; the softer colors *present* the central photo. On the page opposite one simple punched design frame created in three different color schemes offers completely different effects and elicits totally different responses from the viewer.

In addition to color, you will want to think about texture and layering. What kind of special effects will you use? What technique—quilting, quilling, pierced paper, torn paper, punching, stamping, a single photo, several photos, etc. This is a time to have fun, to experiment, to be creative.

▲ DUTCH ART FRAMES, ARTWORK: PAM METZGER, BOULDER, COLORADO

It's great fun to work with punches. Here we have used a few simple shapes sparingly to provide charming frames for three quite different traditional photographs.

(ABOVE LEFT) Bright, primary hues command a sense of elementary fun! (Photo: Megan Brockbank, San Diego, California)

(ABOVE CENTER) Two shades of blue give the punched shape a cool, monochromatic feel. (Photo: Karen Gerbrandt, Broomfield, Colorado)

(ABOVE RIGHT) Deep red, black, burnt umbers, and goldenrod lend a timeless, classic touch.

◄ TYLER AND MARCI, NANCY SCHROEDER, YORK, MAINE

Once again we see the powerful effectiveness of one simple central photograph surrounded by simple decorations. In this case the fern-like green leaves are touched up with a black pen, the tan flower-petal decorated background paper supports the lush flowers in the featured image, and the gorgeous pink hydrangea is a perfect finishing touch.

Generations
of Family

Gaetino
and
Carmela

create a
beautiful
family

Theresa,
Louis and Ann

Louis with Gary
and Carmel

Theresa with John Jr.,
Bill and Steve

Ann & Carlo with
Chuck and Carol

October 3, 1915

1927

1954

▲ GENERATIONS OF FAMILY, CHERYL THOMAS, HIGHLAND, CALIFORNIA

Here, a well-thought-out and beautifully executed scrapbook page of a family tree demonstrates the artist's perceptive sense of color and texture. The leaves punched from soft, unusual "leaf" colors cascade very dramatically against the dark background. The bark-like crinkled, layered paper of the trunk and branches adds texture and depth to the page. Craft wire adds to the texture. Mats cut with decorative-edged scissors present the simply cropped images without fanfare. Minimal, attractive, handwritten journaling completes the page. The photos are simple, the presentation stunning.

Yassky Family Passage from Russia

The Yassky family migrated from Belarouse, Russia because they were persecuted for their religious beliefs. Many years later their Great Great Grandson ran for office and got to meet President Clinton.

In America, the Yasskys were free to celebrate religious traditions, such as a barmitzvah, from the 1950's.

1998 looking back at their success during a Yassky family reunion.

AN AMERICAN DREAM

Dreams can be short term or long term. This page celebrates and rejoices in the good lives of an American family. Not too long ago— just a few generations, in fact— the forbears of the handsome young politician seen shaking hands with President Clinton in the White House emigrated from Russia in search of a better life in the United States.

—*Artwork: Erikia Ghumm, Brighton, Colorado, Photos: Ellin Yassky*

WORKING WITH TEMPLATES

We have included in this book many different techniques from the past to demonstrate both diversity and continuity. Quilting and scrapbooking have much in common. And scrapbookers love to adapt other craft techniques to their own. The technique is basically the same. What is most exciting to scrapbookers is that each quilt pattern can be adapted to complement the photos. Changing the color of the pattern can make it fit your photo and/or color scheme. The patterns themselves are largely composed of various geometric shapes arranged in countless appealing ways. Quilters rarely work without the help of templates —they help to give patterns their crisp, clean, uniform shapes and edges. Templates are just one of the many tools that scrapbookers have borrowed from these fabric artists.

POSITIVE TEMPLATES—To work with positive templates, simply place the template on your paper and trace around the outside edges. Next, cut along the line you've drawn. Because you can't see through these templates, it is easiest to use them on solid colored paper. They may be difficult to place perfectly on a patterned sheet.

NEGATIVE TEMPLATES—A negative template is usually made of paper or plastic, and the interior of the template shape is cut out. With this type of template, you can see exactly what your shaped image will look like after you cut it. Negative templates are great for cropping photos or for selecting a specific pattern in a printed paper. Move the template around until it is positioned over just the section of the photo or paper that you want. Trace the interior edges of the shape, and then cut your photo or paper to its finished size.

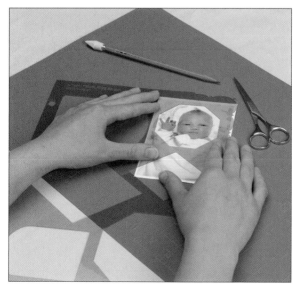

MAKE YOUR OWN TEMPLATES—Quilting books are full of patterns that scrapbookers can use to make templates. You'll need tracing paper and a light board. Trace around the quilting template and cut out the shape. Now, trace this pattern onto cardboard or other sturdy stock or onto stencil film (if you want a see-through template). Decide whether you want a negative or positive template. If you want a positive template, cut along the outline of the shape. If you want a negative template, cut out the interior of the shape.

Photos: Debra Fee, Broomfield, Colorado

◄ AUNT ELIZA'S STAR, ARTWORK: ERIKIA GHUMM, BRIGHTON, COLORADO, PHOTO: LORA MASON, WINTER PARK, FLORIDA

Aunt Eliza's star pattern works for three very different-looking pages. Varying the color schemes and the patterned papers complements the colors in the photographs—birthday, Christmas, and baby's first year.

September 7, 1968

Kathleen Paula Kennedy

◄ KATHLEEN
PAULA KENNEDY,
AMANDA WILSON,
COLORADO SPRINGS,
COLORADO

Every wedding photo is a one-of-a-kind, and this lovely bride's classic origami frame encircles this memorable portrait in a stunning wreath. Beautiful papers folded and assembled together add a third-dimensional richness to an already important photo.

PAPER FOLDING

What more perfect complement to your paper scrapbook page than embellishments made of folded paper? With just a few folds and creases, a two-dimensional composition becomes a strong three-dimensional statement. The "kite" fold explained below is the basic form for the wreath that Amanda Wilson, of Colorado Springs, Colorado, created to frame this beautiful formal bridal portrait. The composition may look complicated, but it is simply sixteen folded squares layered in a circle.

To assemble the wreath, hold two finished pieces with closed points facing the same direction, then slide one piece into the space between the kite and flap of the other piece. Position the pieces so that the closed point of the inserted kite covers half of the wing of the other piece. Layer the folds around the circle. For this page, layer the kite folds around a 4 ¹/₂-inch circle.

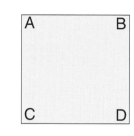

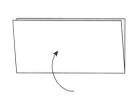

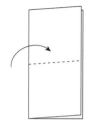

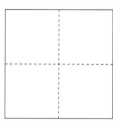

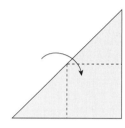

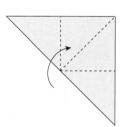

1. Start with a square of paper.

2. With pattern side facing up, fold C and D to A and B, and crease.

3. Open flat, fold A and C to B and D, and crease.

4. Open flat and turn paper over with pattern side down.

5. Bring A to D, forming a triangle, and crease.

6. Open flat, fold C to B, forming a triangle, and crease.

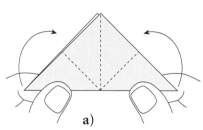

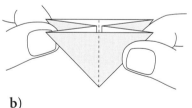

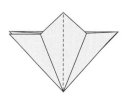

7. (a) Holding folded corners in either hand, push fingers toward center, forming a pocket opening,

(b) then move the corner in your left hand to the back and the one in your right hand to the front, forming a layered triangle as shown.

8. Bring top right flap perpendicular to center fold.

9. Use a pencil to open the edges of raised flap.

10. Keeping center creases aligned, remove the pencil and press flat, creasing both sides of the new kite shape. Turn the piece over and repeat.

▸ MOM AND HER FRIEND CHERYL, ARTWORK: PAM KLASSEN, WESTMINSTER, COLORADO, PHOTO: JOYCE HANSEN, LITTLETON, COLORADO

Working with vellum offers many ways to add an elegant or whimsical finishing touch to your project. Here, torn layers of colored and patterned vellum fill out the chorus. The treatment is fun-loving and upbeat.

▸ CHILI BABY, REBECCA HANSON, GILBERT, ARIZONA

Rebecca took several photos of her daughter wearing a chili pepper costume and then silhouetted the photos and gathered them together to make a strand of chilis. The knot at the top of the chili pepper strand is cut from tan paper.

▴ MOM'S WEDDING, LINDA STRAUSS, PROVO, UTAH

Handmade, rose-strewn paper provides the support for this timeless photograph of young bride and attendant. The soft paper corners gently lift the photo off the page.

▴ OUR FAMILY CHRISTMAS 1997, ARTWORK: ERIKIA GHUMM, BRIGHTON, COLORADO, PHOTOS: SANDRA ESCOBEDO, MANTECA, CALIFORNIA

A solid green tree and festive gifts under the tree are festooned with cut strips of patterned vellum in several colors. A paper crimper gives texture to the vellum. Freehand cut stars and hearts, also of patterned vellum, complete the family holiday picture.

◀ MY WEDDING SHOWER, ANNETTE GRYMONPRE, TALLAHASSEE, FLORIDA

When creating a scrapbook for her wedding shower, the bride-to-be selected a favorite appliqué quilt motif. This creative and complex-looking title page is made up of only four shapes—a leaf, flower, heart, and circle. The umbrella in the center reinforces the scrapbook theme. The hearts are punched. The page is also accented with a mat cut with fancy scissors. Stylized images and a bold heading contribute to a strong graphic presentation.

▶ HEART QUILT, MARILYN GARNER, SAN DIEGO, CALIFORNIA

A scrapbook page with definite attitude, embracing three passions: family, quilting, and scrapbooking itself. The charming photos cropped and matted to fit inside the appliqué flower shapes and arranged in a heart shape let you know this is a well-loved family.

▶ OUR FAMILY, MARTY MUELLER, EDEN PRAIRIE, MINNESOTA

A title page adds a special finishing touch to your scrapbook. Add journaling of names and dates or meaningful verses to make your scrapbook uniquely your own. The images for this page were created with punches on a precut laser die-cut mat and then assembled into a striking wreath. The beautifully handwritten poem (author unknown) describes the essence of family.

► THE GAME OF LIFE, JOANNA SMITH, ALTAMONTE SPRINGS, FLORIDA

The inspiration for this timeline that records the life of this scrapbooker's father—from babyhood to parenthood—came from the classic board game, "Game of Life." A gameboard created from brightly colored cut paper provides the base for wonderful photos cropped and layered on its route. Stickers and simple journaling bring the board to life.

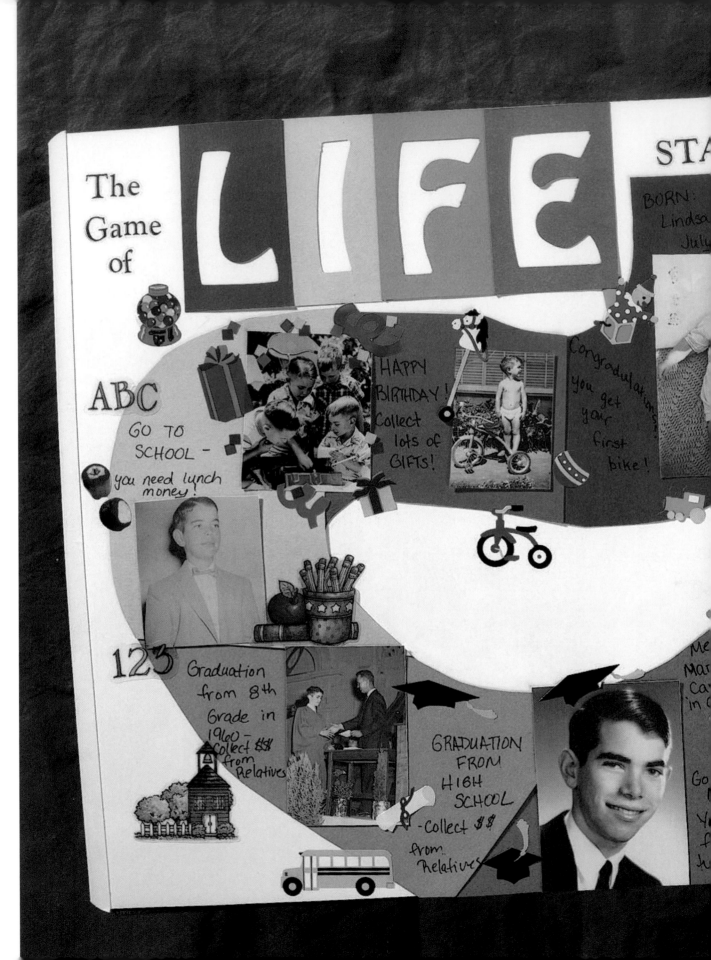

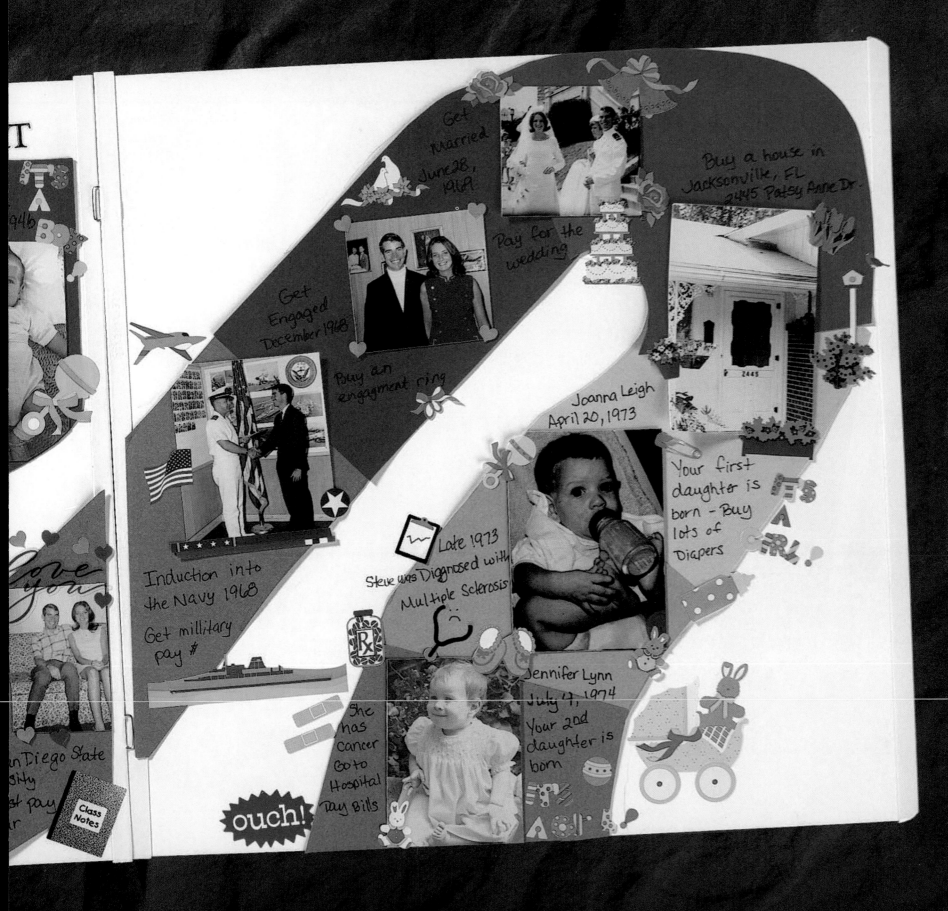

Hyrum and Maria Jensen Olsen - Wedding Day
LDS Logan Temple, Utah - March 6, 1895

YESTERDAY: CELEBRATING YOUR HERITAGE

*A*s we travel from yesterday into tomorrow, from generation to generation, our scrapbooks tell the stories of our lives. With pictures and words, we record our fondest memories and celebrate our connection to the past. Scrapbooks inspire us to reach across time, to rediscover our heritage and our traditions, and to retell our most treasured family stories.

The pages of your scrapbook capture the spirit, faces, and voices of your ancestors—whether they lived long ago or in the recent past. With a little creativity and some of the objects that you have tucked away through the years—portraits, old letters, bits of heirloom lace—you can bring your family's story to life. Create a family tree, journal the funny stories Grandma used to tell you, interview Uncle Lou about what life was like when he was a boy.

Preserve all the memories that matter to you most. The story you tell will be as unique as the people who lived it. What will make your book special to future generations are those small details—the little-known facts about family and friends, the heartfelt traditions, the festive holiday events, and the favorite stories that make these people and places live in your memory. As you build your scrapbook, you'll feel the sense of your own identity deepen—as an individual and as part of a family. You'll develop a new sense of pride in your heritage as you create a strong bond with the past and tie to the future.

◄ HYRUM AND MARIA, LAURIE NELSON CAPENER, PROVIDENCE, UTAH

With touches of gold against a monochromatic color scheme, this heritage wedding page emphasizes the dignity of this couple and their solemn intent. The laser die-cut mat adds an additional touch of Old World elegance.

▲ SIX GENERATIONS, NICOLE RAMSAROOP, HORST, THE NETHERLANDS

Nicole made this heritage quilt page for her daughter. She collected the old photographs from her great-aunt in Holland—the oldest living member of her family.

The past gives shape to our lives today. It is also the foundation on which the next generations build their future. What better place to begin a family scrapbook than with the stories of the people that came before us? As the older members of the family grow older, we realize the importance of preserving their stories and memories. How many times the world over have children begged "Tell me a story, Grandpa, tell me about 'the olden days'?" Take that opportunity now and present those stories in your own visually meaningful way.

FAMILY TREE, ARTWORK: ERIKIA GHUMM, BRIGHTON, COLORADO; PHOTOS: MARY ANNE DENNEY, LAKEWOOD, COLORADO

Make a family tree to record the names, dates, and places of birth, death, and marriage of relatives. You can fill the "branches" in many imaginative ways. Family lines are usually quite long. The "leaves" of this handcut-paper tree present a lot of information in an appealing and space-efficient way.

▲ ROOTS AND BRANCHES, Joy Carey, Visalia, California

To make it easy to update her computer-generated genealogies, this scrapbooker mounts the page with clear photo mounts. When she wants to update her information, she simply removes the old page and inserts the new one. The printed page is matted on dark green paper, which is mounted on a pale green parchment background.

◀ FAMILY TREE, Lisa Jackson, San Antonio, Texas

This family tree is just one page in an entire album created as a remembrance of Lisa's grandmother's 100th birthday celebration. Leaf die cuts, photos, ribbon, and rose stickers make a brightly colored tree that blooms with the memory of loved ones.

DAVEY FAMILY TREE

I had some photos in hand when I accepted the challenge to create a family tree scrapbook page. The year before, I had gone to the Davey family reunion for the first time. Davey is my father's mother's maiden name. I met her sister, Dorothy, there and we hit it off immediately. She has done a lot of research on the family, and provided most of the photographs. The style and color palette I chose for the page did not come easily. I wanted to do something different, something special. I love art deco so I started there. I found a 1930 paper photo frame that I had received from my grandmother, and then came up with the red rhinestones to use as leaves. They sparkled like gems, and that's how I felt about the photos and learning about my family. They are gems to me. — *Erikia Ghumm, Brighton, Colorado*

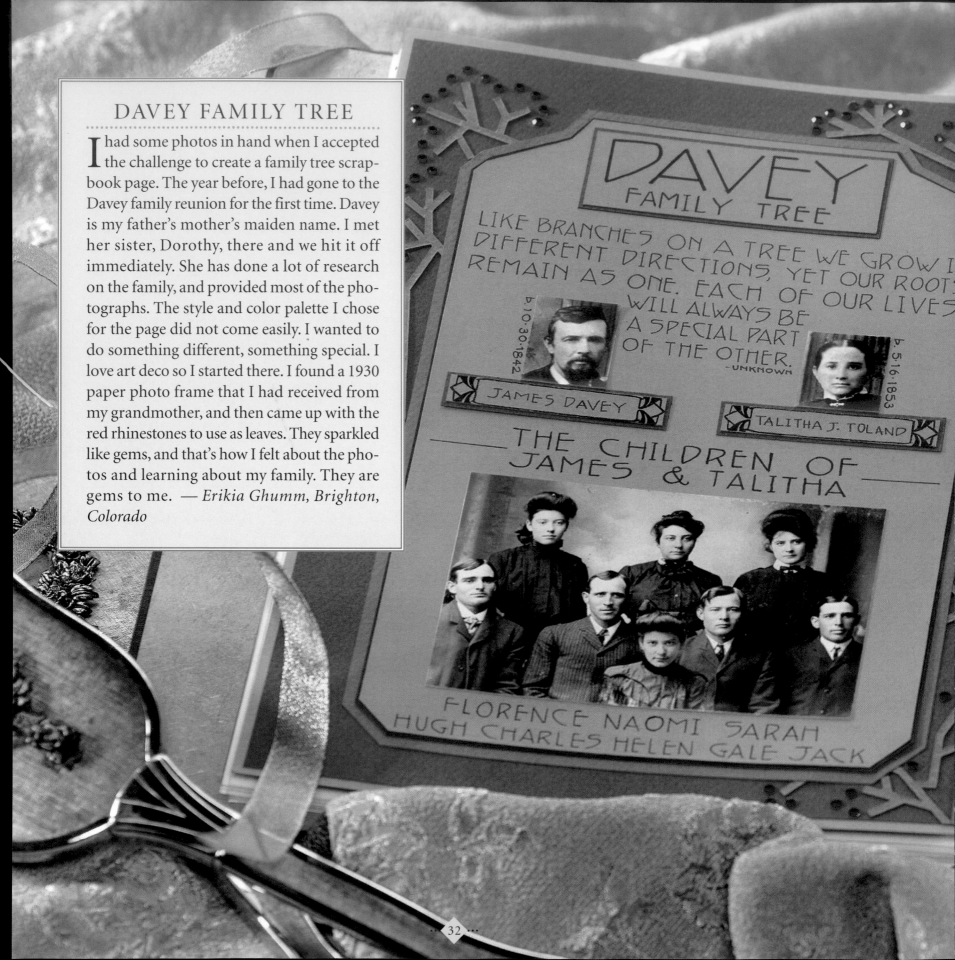

DAVEY FAMILY TREE

LIKE BRANCHES ON A TREE WE GROW IN DIFFERENT DIRECTIONS, YET OUR ROOTS REMAIN AS ONE. EACH OF OUR LIVES WILL ALWAYS BE A SPECIAL PART OF THE OTHER. — UNKNOWN

b. 10-30-1842

JAMES DAVEY

b. 5-16-1853

TALITHA J. TOLAND

THE CHILDREN OF JAMES & TALITHA

FLORENCE NAOMI SARAH
HUGH CHARLES HELEN GALE JACK

b·1·20·1875 — W. GALE DAVEY

b·11·11·1888 — HILDEGARDE A. POULSEN

THE CHILDREN OF GALE & HILDEGARD

b·5·31·1910 — A. FERN DAVEY

b·12·20·1925 — W. GALE DAVEY JR.

b·2·22·1917 — DOROTHY D. DAVEY

b·10·3·1922 — ALBERT A. DAVEY

b·1·23·1913 — ROSE L. DAVEY

b·1·16·1915 — CHARLES J. DAVEY

b·3·25·1908 — R. EUGENE DAVEY

Leisure Time at the Turn of the Century

THE MC CORMICK FAMILY 1903
NEWPORT, R.I.

LILLIAN & HAROLD
ALL DRESSED UP TO
MAKE A SNOWMAN.

FANCY A GAME OF TENNIS? MY GRANDMOTHER
AND GREAT AUNT.

NO NEED FOR SUNSCREEN.
MC CORMICK FAMILY TRIP
TO THE BEACH.

A LOVELY
SUMMER DAY.
1906

TURN-OF-THE-CENTURY FAMILY

When my mother died a few years ago, her twin sister, the only remaining sibling of their family of five, brought down from her attic several boxes of old family photos and asked if I'd like to go through them while she could still identify everyone! Some of the people I knew, some I didn't, some had died before I was born. The feelings emanating from the photos were warm and congenial, and quietly celebratory. My aunt's lovely smile widened as she remembered the moments: children showing off their just-created snowman to their father; grandmother taking some children for a ride in a jaunty horse and buggy; an adults' winter Sunday afternoon walk on the beach carrying an adored first child; a tennis game at home; Aunt Lilly, coquettish, with a "beau." What a treat. —*Ellen Brunelle, artwork: Erikia Ghumm, Brighton, Colorado*

MY GRANDFATHER, WILLIAM MAHER

I tracked down a journal I had heard of that had been written by a great-grandfather, born in 1840 in Quebec, Canada. "My Journal and History of My Life," it read, "the Days of My Childhood, the Rambles and Pleasures of My Boyhood Days, the Death of My Parents, My Departure from Home, My Travels through Canada and the United States, and Three Years in the Army." Begun in 1866, the worn, yellowed pages in rather arch handwriting read like a nineteenth-century novel: large happy family, parents die young, children separated, walking from Quebec to Chicago at the age of fourteen, finding work, joining the Army, etc. I don't even remember having seen a photograph of him before. Reading his journal made him come alive. The journal itself was incomplete; it just trailed off as he went to fight in the Civil War. At the end, though, were some pages with a price list of plants that he, then a landscape gardener and florist, offered for sale in the spring of 1875. It was like a door opening. The plant list today is very much the same, though the prices differ slightly.

—*Maria Barry, artwork: Erikia Ghumm, Brighton, Colorado*

QUILTING

LAZY DAISY QUILT PATTERN

One of the nicest aspects of scrapbooking is the opportunity it presents to include ideas and techniques from other crafts. Quilting has always been an important craft and quilt patterns are a popular motif with scrapbookers. Quilt patterns can be adapted to create beautiful borders, frames, or even the central motif on a large page.

This Lazy Daisy quilt-style page combines a patchwork motif and a distinctive style of raised "stitching" called trapunto. The star and chevron patches are made with diamonds cut from red and blue cardstock. The "stitching" pattern is made by tracing a feather pattern on a lightbox.

1. Using the chevron template on page 140, enlarge if necessary, trace, and cut out twenty-four red and twenty-four blue cardboard diamonds.

2. Carefully cut the diamonds out. Be accurate; the diamonds need to fit together neatly to form a star, but if they don't, you can trim them later.

3. Crop your photo to a round shape with a template, about 3½ inches in diameter. Find the center of your scrapbook page by drawing diagonals from corner to corner lightly with a pencil and ruler. Center the photo on the page.

Assemble the stars in each of the corners, carefully placing diamonds of alternating colors to make the shape. Next, make two chevrons between each star to form the border.

To create the effect of raised trapunto stitching, use a lightbox and a light tan pen to trace the feather pattern around the center photo. "Stitch" a crosshatch pattern in the squares in the border with the same pen. Add shadowing within the feather pattern using tan chalk and a cotton swab.

With a pen, add "stitching" lines around the inside edges of the red and blue diamonds. Add a title or journaling to the page.

▶ THE BEAR FAMILY 1897, JOY CAREY, VISALIA, CALIFORNIA

A descendant of the Bear family combined quilting traditions of the mid-nineteenth century—the Lazy Daisy patchwork pattern and trapunto stitching, a raised design technique—to create this frame for a vintage family portrait.

The Bear Family

1897

Charlie Rogers

Elmer Hatch

Newaygo County, Michigan

1898

LOG CABIN QUILT PATTERN

The logic and format of quilting lends itself readily to scrapbookers. What you can do with fabric you can do with paper. We feature adaptations of three distinctive quilt patterns in this book, showing the variety of treatments that are possible in the creation of your scrapbook pages. And somehow, that connection to the past—to the past of quilters—adds a further dimension to the creation of our own scrapbook pages.

Four Log Cabin quilt blocks serve as the background for the photograph of—naturally—lumberjacks! The basic block of this design is called the Spiraling Log Cabin. To create shading, dark-print papers are used on one half of the block, and light-print papers on the other.

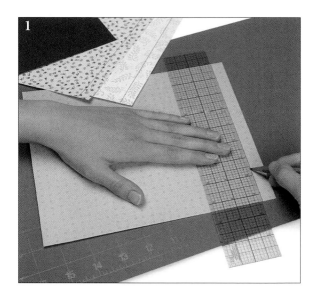

1. Choose a variety of light and dark printed papers. Use a ruler and pencil to mark thirty-two strips, $1/2$ inch wide, on the light-print paper and thirty-two strips of the same width on the dark-print paper.

2. Cut out the strips with a scissors or use the ruler and a craft knife to cut the strips on a flat, protected surface. Divide your scrapbook page into quarters, drawing lines with the ruler and pencil.

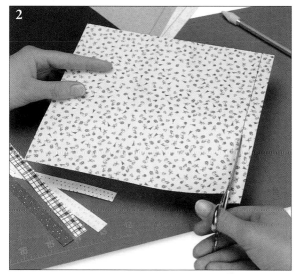

3. Work with the template on page 140 to create a block in each quarter of the page. Dark strips are positioned in the shaded areas and light strips in the unshaded areas. Glue down the light strips first, working from the center of the page. Finish one block before starting the next.

When the blocks are finished, glue a 2-inch red square at the center of each one. Crop and double-mat your photograph with black and white papers. Make the mats very narrow so they don't hide too much of the quilt background. Add journaling to the red squares at the center of the blocks.

◄ SPIRALING LOG CABIN, Debra Fee, Broomfield, Colorado
. . . .

Using strips of various colored printed paper, the Log Cabin pattern is a popular design for quilters and scrapbookers alike. The pattern begins with one square in the center around which strips or long, narrow rectangles are arranged. Frequently, as with this page, the Log Cabin quilts featured a red square in the center to symbolize the hearth as the center of the home. The structure of the four basic tan, black, red, and white pieced blocks supports a wonderful black-and-white photograph of two hardworking lumberjacks.

PETER THIESSEN FAMILY 1917
IN OCTOBER 1917 PETER THIESSEN WAS A WIDOWER. HE HAD
NINE CHILDREN AND TWENTY SEVEN GRAND CHILDREN.

▲ PETER THIESSEN FAMILY 1917, ARTWORK: ERIKIA GHUMM, BRIGHTON, COLORADO, PHOTOS: ALMA FRANZ, INMAN, KANSAS

Studio group portraits with their warm and inviting colors invoke sweet memories of bygone days. Here a simple classic proscenium frames the formal family portrait in muted colors. Journaling along the bottom of the page names the widower Peter Thiessen—father of nine and grandfather of twenty-seven.

CREATING YOUR FAMILY ARCHIVES

Begin your research by contacting as many relatives as you can and telling them about your interest. Everyone has his or her own story, and the more relatives you find, the more history you'll uncover.

Obtain and begin to fill out ancestor charts or family group charts. You can find these basic forms in books, at genealogy societies, and library genealogy departments. Or start with a simple list. Begin with yourself and work back generation by generation, filling in names and dates for each family member as you gather the information.

Be sure you can verify the information you collect. Don't overlook the official documents you may already have at home—certificates of birth, marriage, and death—and the more informal records, such as report cards, family Bibles, obituaries in newspapers, wedding programs, and so on. Ask your relatives to do the same. It's a good idea to transcribe any audio or videotaped interviews since these tapes have limited lifespans. Any information you are missing may be on record in local county offices—real estate deeds, wills, military pensions, for example.

Find out about genealogy at the library and contact local genealogical societies in your area. The research process can be overwhelming, and the support of others with similar interests can be very helpful.

Respect the privacy of the living. You may well come upon family problems or colorful facts about your ancestors that would be hurtful to some living relatives if uncovered. And don't give out too many details on Web sites. The whereabouts of some family members might best not be made public for various reasons.

DIGITAL RESTORATION

Digital restoration is one way to preserve old photographs—without their imperfections! A professional photo finisher can scan the photo, repair any visible tears or discoloration, and print out the image at whatever size you need for your scrapbook page. To make sure you always have a copy of the photograph, ask the photo lab to store the corrected image for you on a disc. Store the disc at home in a safe place.

WORKING WITH HISTORIC PHOTOS

For an archival-quality album environment:
- *Assume all memorabilia is acidic; never let photos and memorabilia touch.*
- *Use only acid- and lignin-free papers, photo-safe adhesives, and pigment inks.*
- *Handle photos with care, avoiding direct light.*
- *Use nonpermanent mounting techniques (photo corners, sleeves, etc.) for easy removal for copying or restoration.*
- *Keep cropping to a minimum; background objects tell their own stories of place and time.*
- *Don't trim or hand-tint old photos; have reprints made first.*

Artwork: Debbie Mock, Littleton, Colorado

Several times each summer either prairie hay or alfalfa is cut with a horse-drawn mower and left to dry on the ground.

Then it is raked into piles with a horse-drawn dump rake. Each time you lift the lever to dump a load you get a hit on the seat.

These piles are then picked up with an implement called a go-devil. When it is full it is lifted slightly, brought to the stack and then dumped.

These stacks are feed for the livestock in the winter months when pastures are dry. These photos date back to 1909.

▲ HAYING TIME, ARTWORK: ERIKIA GHUMM, BRIGHTON, COLORADO, PHOTOS: ALMA FRANZ, INMAN, KANSAS

Erikia was given the photos and story for this page. The photos themselves actually tell the story of harvest time, summer 1909, on a Kansas farm. A dark green barn-siding background sets the stage for the series of photos bordered with black marker and the starkly simple wagon wheel. The earth-toned straightforward presentation reflects the strength of the hard-working men. Hand-cut paper elements reflect the time when things were hand made.

DADDY AND FRIENDS

College men enjoying life to the fullest, from playing in the college band to Uncle Jake sledding with friends. The geometric pattern of layered paper in a bold palette supports this lively "slice-of-life" view of early-twentieth-century Kansas.
—*Artwork: Erikia Ghumm, Brighton, Colorado*

Augustus J. Sininger (later Sitinger) born in Baden-Baden, Germ. lived 85 years. Married 1846 Catharine Beirley Sininger 1817-1883, born in Wurtemburg, Germ. Immigrated in 1837. He was a skilled mechanic and invented a part for the cotton gin (a blower or vacuum to separate ball from seed). 11 children. Gave each child when married a farm from land purchased in two counties(ohio).

John A. Sininger 7.20.1859-1939, 79 years. Miriam Lou Miller Sininger 1.7.1867-1959, 92 years. 11 children. She always was patient and kind, and had time to visit. Lived on wedding gift farm til sold at death.

Mary Isabelle Sininger Robinson "Granny" born 11.5.1899. William Coleman Robinson "Poke" 9.9.1894-1978. 5 children. 1923 Moved from Ohio to Oklahoma, banks failed during sale & purchase of farm & lost all. In 1936 sent kids a postcard to meet in Bernice September going to California.

Truman John Robinson 4.29.1916-2000, 83 years old. Married 2.9.1935 Ruth Maurine Martin Robinson. September 1936 came west. Phyliss was 9 mo., living in 1 room cabin, no steady work except haying. Settled in Longview, WA. A local man hired on at Weyerhauser 2 weeks after arriving and camping on lake bank. Retired from Weyerhauser. 2 children, Phyliss & John.

John William Robinson 9.23.1939 Diane Marie Eddy Robinson 2.18.1942 Diane remarried. Divorced 1980. Each remarried. Jackie Tecla Robinson Steven Gennuso

Wendi Marie Robinson Hitchings 12.11.1960 Steven Allen Hitchings 1.27.1957 Married 9.12.1981. 3 children Alina, Ellie, & Mae

John & Miriam Sininger and their farm in Ohio.

Poke Robinson's sale notice of 1936. All Robinson history lost when his parent's farmhouse burnt to the ground. Sisters squabbling over ownership. Only family heirloom/history is a large wooden chest (the Robinsons used when immigrated in 1908 from Holland.)

PUBLIC SALE

Having decided to move to another state, I will offer for sale at Public Auction, all my Live Stock, Farming Tools and Household Goods, at the Oyler farm 1 mile northwest of Grove, on the

Wednesday, Aug. 26th

starting promptly at 10:00 A.M. on

W. C. ROBINSON, Owner
DAVID REEVES, Auct.

Mommie, where do we come from?

William H. Clark 9.10.1833-1898, 65 years Jane Davis 12.12.1830. 7 children. He served in Civil War. A very happy family.

Margaret Jane Clark McPherson 4.24.1846-8.5.1924, 66 years William E. McPherson 4.10.1846-1929, 83 years 7 children. He served in Civil War and told lots of war stories. He enjoyed photo developing.

Karen Happuch McPherson Martin 7.13.1887 Frank Ernest Martin 5.16.1999. Divorced 2 children. Owned grocery store. Family enjoyed Sundays in Tulsa window shopping.

Ruth Maurine Martin Robinson 1.25.1919, vibrant 81 year old!

Margaret Jane Clark McPherson grew up (4-18 years) on this farm. In 1878 family moved to 160 acre farm in Oswego, Kansas.

Frank & Karen Martin My Grandma Ruth giggles at this picture of her parents with her Dad's pants rolled up. He loved nice clothes and always dressed sharp.

Karen Happuch McPherson Martin Born 7.13.1887

Frank Earnest born 5.16

PUBLIC SALE

These simple black-and-white pages reflect the quiet dignity of a farming life in the story of a Dutch immigrant family and their move west. The family farm in Oklahoma was put up for public sale in August 1936 because the father "decided to move to another state." All Robinson family history was lost when the parents' farmhouse burned to the ground. —*Wendi Hitchings, Issaquah, Washington*

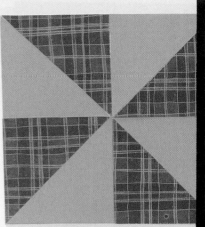

Burton Lee Pegg
- born November 24, 1873
- died February 17, 1929
- married Edna May Hatch
  February 25, 1914

Lee, as everyone called him, was seventeen years older than Edna. He was a friend of one of her brothers.

Lee died in a factory accident at the Henry Street plant of the Campbell Wyant and Cannon Foundry in Muskegon, Michigan. His coat got caught in a revolving mill, and when he was thrown into a pile of metal castings, he fractured a vertebrae in the lower part of his spine. He is buried in Woodland Cemetery in Reed City.

MAN'S LIFE

Burton Lee Pegg (1837–1929) was thrown to his death in a foundry accident when his coat caught in a revolving mill. The strong, simple quilt pattern frames the central images in a home-spun pattern that reflects the gentle strength of the man and the poignancy of his story. —*Debra Fee, Broomfield, Colorado*

Three Generations of
Rinaldi Family
Recipes and Memories

Kim age 5 - always
gets the first scoop!

This recipe
Rinaldi fam
for over 5
Great Aunt Em
to use leftover pea
family orchard in

Country Peach ice (

1 T. lemon juice
2 eggs
½ cup yogurt
1 cup brown sugar, packed firmly
1 t. vanilla
10-12 ripe peaches, peeled, pitted and quartered
2 cups cream

Blend juice, eggs, yogurt, sugar and vanilla in
processor or blender until smooth.
Add fruit. Blend until only small pieces remain.
Add cream. Pour mixture into ½ gallon ice cream
freezer.
Freeze according to manufacturer's directions.
To serve top with fresh peach slices.

▲ THREE GENERATIONS OF RECIPES AND MEMORIES, KATHY STELIGO, SAN CARLOS, CALIFORNIA

Kathy has turned her passion for both food and scrapbooking into a meaningful way to preserve her family heritage—and her mother-in-law's favorite recipes!

PRESERVING FAMILY RECIPES

Scrapbookers don't have to be limited in the way they express their creativity, or their family history. Taking a look at your family's history through *your* eyes is fun and rewarding. What is *your* passion? Look at the family stories, celebrations, remembrances in that light. Do you love art, travel, theater, science, fishing, food? Find your favorite themes in your family's story and make the connections. Find a common thread. So much of our lives centers around food. Family recipes is a natural. Keepsake cookbooks combine favorite family recipes and family traditions.

Kathy Steligo of Carlos, California, a "fanatic scrapbooker and a fanatic cook," was always looking for a way to combine the two. Working side-by-side in the kitchen with her Sicilian mother-in-law, something clicked. "Every time I would cook with her, she told me wonderful stories about how she remembered cooking the same thing with her mother. It struck me that these recipes and stories were an important part of her heritage." The pages in Kathy's albums include more than just ingredients and measurements, they are also filled with photos and journaling relating to each favorite dish.

Kathy decided to compile her mother-in-law's favorite recipes into a keepsake recipe album. To record the recipes, her mother-in-law prepared each dish while Kathy measured quantities. The dishes were prepared a little differently each time because her mother-in-law never measures ingredients. With the use of a tape recorder and a home computer, Kathy documented the stories associated with each recipe using large, easy-to-read type. To get started, it's best to choose a theme, collect the recipes, record food memories, and add photos and any other illustrations.

Keepsake cookbooks make perfect gifts. Some of our fondest memories involve food. Document your family recipes along with stories, photos, and traditions. A lot of families pass things down word-of-mouth, but after one or two generations, a lot of detail gets lost. Too many people say, "I wish I had that recipe from my mother," or, "I wish I could remember that story about Grandma's fried chicken." Although the thought of assembling a large cookbook might be mind-boggling, an easy way to get started is to incorporate recipe pages in your family scrapbooks.

A very successful recipe book was one we made for a bridal shower. Each guest was asked to contribute a recipe. Each spread in the book includes a recipe and a photo of the bride with the recipe-giver, along with extra shower pictures.

Whether to type recipes or handwrite them is a matter of preference and convenience. The handwritten recipes in our recipe book add to the personal nature of the gift. Sometimes, however, it may not be practical to complete a recipe album entirely by hand. If you plan to make multiple copies of the book, you might seriously consider typing the recipes on the computer, if you don't want to have copies made of the handwritten pages.

FAMILY FAVORITES

When mother died, several of us gathered at her house to get things in order. Ann took a box of old papers and photos. That year, each of the siblings received a remarkable Christmas gift—a silver box (metal CD case, actually) wrapped with a vellum band announced *Family Favorites: Good Times, Good Thoughts, Good Food*. Each box contained a selection of favorite family recipes printed on vellum and copies of wonderful old photographs of each family member, mostly on their birthday when the tradition was to have your photograph taken while holding your homemade-by-Mom birthday cake. We had lots of family traditions—the birthday photo with cake, Dad's best-ever homegrown popcorn, hot chocolate every Sunday morning after church, Christmas popcorn balls. And Ann captured the best for us. Dad's popcorn *was* extraordinary. Every night, long after supper, we would gather around the kitchen table and share a giant pot of homegrown popcorn and family tales. Dad grew the corn, dried the kernels, and popped the corn. We had the fun of eating it. I've never tasted better popcorn. The photo on the right shows Ann pouring melted butter on a fresh batch. After Mom and Dad sold the farm and moved closer to town, Ann, then married and living farther north in Minnesota, decided to grow some corn, dry it, and give the kernels to Dad for Christmas so he could continue the family tradition of real homegrown popcorn. All went well until she went into the attic to collect the dried kernels, only to find that the mice had beaten her to it. Needless to say, we didn't have real homegrown popcorn that Christmas. I had no idea that a bunch of old photos and recipes would bring so many memories flooding back. How wonderful that I can actually *see* the church suppers and picnics with Mom's famous bars—chocolate, Rice Krispies (of course), and scotcheroos! No self-respecting proper Minnesotan would visit anyone's home or picnic without a batch or two! —*Judy Ritchie*

SCOTCHEROOS

Wayne loved these bars and Mom always made sure she had them on hand when we came to Minnesota. My recipe card looks like Wayne started to write it, but Mom finished it (she probably found a job for him to do).

> 1 cup sugar
> 1 cup corn syrup

Combine and bring to a boil, remove from stove, and add:

> 1 cup peanut butter
> 5 cups Rice Krispies

Pour into a well-buttered 9 x 12 cake pan. Put butter on your hands and pat the mixture into the pan. Melt together in a double boiler:

> 1 6-oz. package chocolate chips
> 1 6-oz. package butterscotch chips

Pour this mixture while still warm on top of the peanut butter and Rice Krispie mixture. Refrigerate for a few minutes to set and cool. Cut into bars and serve.

Artwork (facing page): Erikia Ghumm, Brighton, Colorado

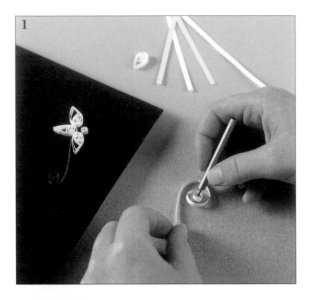

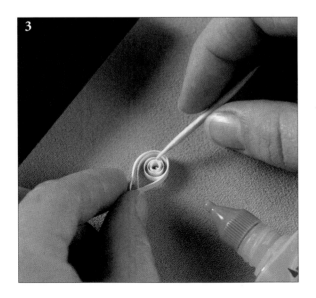

QUILLING

Creative scrapbookers find inspiration in many places. Quilling adds sculptural dimension to your pages. The effect is sophisticated and dramatic. Quilling is a simple decorative technique that you can use to embellish any kind of page—whether it's formal or casual fun. You simply roll thin strips of paper into various shapes and then arrange and combine the shapes to make your design. You can make flower centers and teardrop petals, leaves, scrolls, and stems. You can glue designs together, too, to form borders and garlands of flowers. The standard size for quilling paper is 1/8 inch, but wider and thinner sizes are available, too. You'll also need glue and a slotted or needle tool around which you can roll the paper.

1. Cut a strip of paper to the desired length—shorter for smaller shapes, longer for larger shapes. Moisten one end of the strip and place that end against your index finger. Position the needle tool on the end of the paper. Press the end of the paper around the tool with your thumb. Hold the tool steady and roll the paper, keeping the edges of the strip as even as possible.

2. To make a tight circle, roll the strip around the tool. Slip the tool from the roll's center and hold the roll to keep it from unwinding. Glue the loose end of the paper to the side of the roll. To make a loose circle, simply let the roll loosen slightly when you remove the tool.

3. To make a teardrop leaf, pinch one side of a loose circle to form a point. To make a scroll, roll only one end of the strip and leave the other end loose. To make a V scroll, crease the strip at its center and roll each end away from the crease.

TIP

Remember, when you want to use a quilling technique to create embellishments for your page, the smaller the tool, the tighter the roll. When adding such a dimensional accent to the page, less is definitely more. Small accents are more effective than massive areas of ornamentation.

▶ WEDDING PARTY, AMANDA WILSON, COLORADO SPRINGS, COLORADO

Old wedding photos or group portraits—from every era—invoke sweet memories of bygone days. The delicate quilled embellishments add to the elegance.

Jean K. (Brightman) Camire   Sandra J. Kent   Antoinette Dehullu   Kathleen P. (Kennedy) Wilson   Douglas E. Wilson Jr.   Ronald J. Wilson   Richard D. Kennedy   Harry Briggs III   John E. Wilson Jr.

September 7, 1968
North Parish Church
North Andover, MA

▲ BEAUTIFUL AS A ROSEBUD, PHOTO: CHERYL WINSOR FOR THE MARSHALL COMPANY

Sarah's charming black-and-white portrait comes to life with soft hand-tinted colors, applied sparingly to create a dreamy, nostalgic effect.

HANDCOLORING PHOTOGRAPHS

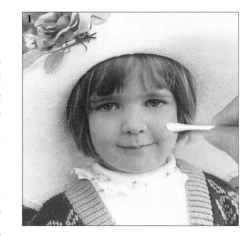

The small finishing touches on a scrapbook page are often what make the page. A gentle touch of color wiped onto black-and-white photos are one most attractive way to refine the finished product. Black-and-white photos can be beautifully and subtly enhanced by a soft tint of color applied sparingly, and a new photo can be give an "aged" look when touched with a hint of hand coloring.

You can add soft, hand-tinted color to any of your black-and-white or sepia-tone photographs. Be sure that the photo has a matte or semi-matte finish. If you would rather not work on the original photographs—particularly old, one-of-a-kind photographs—have the photo lab make reprints or make copies on a color copying machine. Choose photo oil color paints in the colors you'll need—white, red, blue, black, yellow—and any other colors that appeal to you. You won't need much paint, so buy small tubes.

Squirt a small amount of each color you want to use on tracing paper, wax paper, or palette paper. You'll also need cotton balls, cotton swabs, and toothpicks; a utility knife; and a white, nonabrasive eraser. Put a few sheets of drawing paper underneath your photograph as a cushion.

You can apply color to the whole photograph or to one small area. You can mix any of the colors before you apply them, or blend them on the photo. Subtle colors will create a nostalgic look; stronger colors will be more dramatic.

1. To apply color, put a tiny amount of paint on a cotton swab. Tap off the excess paint. Gently rub the color in the desired area in a circular motion. If you are working on small, detailed areas, wrap the tip of a toothpick with a little cotton to apply the color.

2. If the color is too bright, gently rub the area with a clean cotton ball to tone down the color. The more you rub, the lighter the tint. Don't worry about staying in the "lines." If one color washes over the edge of another, work the first color again in that area.

3. You can also erase photo oils before they dry! To remove color in a large area, simply rub it off with a clean cotton ball. To remove color along edges and in small areas (teeth and eyes, for example), use the edge of a white, nonabrasive erase. (To keep the edge of your eraser sharp as you work, trim it with a utility knife. Clean the eraser from time to time, too, by rubbing it on a clean rag.)

As soon as the oil paint dries, the color is permanent. If you have only lightly tinted the image, you can usually handle the photograph in a few days. If you have applied a lot of paint—and depending on the paper type and humidity—you may have to wait a few weeks before handling the photograph.

▲ DIE CUT WINDOW FRAME, ARTWORK: PAM KLASSEN, WESTMINSTER, COLORADO, PHOTO: MICHELE GERBRANDT

Frames are always important. But frames with a "twist" add extra dimension. Creative scrapbookers add new dimensions with materials and techniques. This scrapbooker has taken a commercially available die-cut frame and created a center-opening window frame by mounting the white frame on black paper and cutting down the center through both layers to form two window halves. Then she cut out the inside edges of each half to form a window through which we see the wedding portrait underneath. Each half of the die-cut window frame is then hinged to the outside edges of the portrait page.

LEGACY

Clare, adopted in China in 2000, has been given a Chinese middle name "DaiXi" to honor Great-Grandmother Daisy, who lived in China in the 1930s as a medical missionary and who loved the country with all her heart. Daisy's spirit will not be forgotten; and her love of China—its beauty and history—will continue for many more generations. —*Melanie Mitchell, Overland Park, Kansas*

September 3, 1934
Mr. and Mrs. Anthony A. Aurelia

▲ **50TH ANNIVERSARY,** Sandra van Heusen, St. Clair Shores, Michigan

To celebrate her in-laws' 50th anniversary, Sandra created a page that compared the popular shows, presidents, and prices in the year the couple got married to the same in the year of their golden anniversary.

▶ **MARRIAGE CERTIFICATE,** Linda Milligan, El Paso, Texas

Historical documents add special interest to your heritage pages. Make photocopies so that you don't damage the originals—which you will want to keep in a safe place. Reduce or enlarge the documents to fit your page.

◀ **ANTHONY AND MARION,** Katherine Aurelia, Kokomo, Indiana

This simple and delicate wedding portrait was matted with green paper and lace-paper stickers and trimmed with a corner rounder punch.

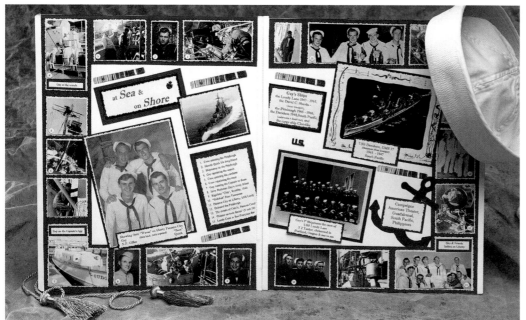

▲ WELCOME HOME JIM,
NANCY CHEARNO-STERSHIC,
BEL AIR, MARYLAND

This patriotic page celebrates the day "Jimmy came home from the war." The vintage photos are matted with red, white, and blue. The stars are punched, and the banner is cut freehand.

◀ AT SEA AND ON SHORE,
LINDA MILLIGAN, EL PASO, TEXAS

Literally rows of simply matted candid snapshots flood the page capturing sailors' lives on land and sea. Journaled captions bring the images all together.

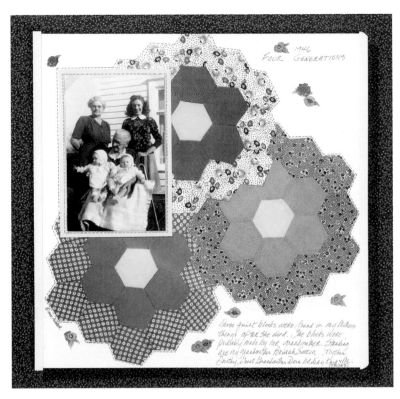

▲ FOUR GENERATIONS, FAYE WEBER, BOISE, IDAHO

When their mother died, Faye and her sister found a box of quilt blocks among her things. The fabrics were from the 1930s and 1940s, and Faye thought the blocks might have been made by her great-grandmother. Faye washed and pressed the blocks and then photocopied them. She arranged the copies into a pieced quilt pattern and added photographs of her twin sister and herself, her mother, grandmother, and great-grandmother. Faye kept the real fabric blocks to later make into a quilt project.

▲ MADE ESPECIALLY FOR ME, JUDY WESTON, POPLAR BLUFF, WISCONSIN

When Judy was a little girl, her grandmother, who lived to be 103 years old, made her a Sunbonnet Sue quilt. Just a few years ago on a trip to New York City, Judy found a Sunbonnet Sue rubber stamp, which she used with colorful inks to decorate this page honoring her grandmother. A photograph of the actual quilt is at the center, surrounded by variously cropped, matted, and framed photographs of Grandmother Moll at various stages of her life .

FIVE GENERATIONS OF YOUNG WOMEN
(following spread)

In a box of photos old and new, we found a portrait of a woman I had never seen before. I had heard stories of the strength of the McCormick women. This photo turned out to be of my mother's mother's mother. There certainly is strength in her face. And then, the appealing image of my mother and her twin sister with their mother in a rather formal studio portrait reiterated the relaxed, casual air my mother possessed, while her sister was ever demure. I couldn't resist adding on photos of my daughter and me. There *is* a line to be traced. Maybe someone in a future generation will continue the line. I'd love to see the progression. —*Ellen Maher, artwork: Erikia Ghumm, Brighton, Colorado*

Five
Generations
of
Young
Women

Margaret 1900

Every baby born into this world is a finer one than the last.
—CHARLES DICKENS

Eileen 1911

Elen 1911

Eunice 1911

Leslie 1943

Maria 1972

each bell was attached to a present

Seth + his friend walter do a craft

Seth in his tree nat

Seths class has a Happy Birthday Jesus party

TODAY: MAKING MEMORIES

W e make memories every day. Some of our most memorable days are special and festive occasions—weddings, birthdays, holiday celebrations. These bright days are full of wonderful foods, lively games, music, and color—and warm and lasting memories for everyone who is there to enjoy them. Most scrapbooks are full of pages that record these happy times in words and pictures.

Most of our days, however, are just ordinary ones—filled with familiar routines. In some ways, these are the days that we remember most fondly. We often take them for granted, but our day-to-day lives are filled with significant moments. In time, these simple memories will be especially meaningful. Our everyday activities reveal the close bonds that we share with other family members—gathered around the dinner table, cooking together in the kitchen, reading a book, caring for someone who is under the weather, building sand castles on the beach.

Perhaps this was the last Thanksgiving you celebrated with an elderly grandparent; or maybe a family member was ill or too far away to join the festivities. Maybe a favorite grandparent told a poignant story showing his or her strength and resolve—a story demonstrating grace in the face of hardship. These, too, are moments you will want to capture and remember. You'll start to see your everyday world in a new light. And if you catch a bit of nostalgia, so much the better.

◀ CHRISTMAS SAMPLER, MARILYN GARNER, SAN DIEGO, CALIFORNIA

The bright colors and playful shapes and accents of this sampler quilt page add a touch of whimsy to holiday school memories. The "stitch" lines are drawn with ink. Crisp, clean Christmas shapes, cut with seasonal templates and filled with appropriately cropped photos, surround a central colorful pieced-paper Santa figure.

▲ THE MEMORIES THAT TOUCH OUR HEARTS, DAWN MABE, BROOMFIELD, COLORADO

Rather than assembling this patchwork-quilt page with glue, Dawn actually stitched the squares together on her sewing machine. Stitching paper will eventually dull your needle, but you can make a few pages before you have to replace it, and it definitely adds authenticity.

THE CHANGING SEASONS

Many scrapbook artists choose the cycle of changing seasons as the organizing theme for their pages. Each of the four seasons has its own color schemes, motifs, holidays, traditions, and activities. The sights and sensations associated with each one of them can provide you with fresh sources of design inspiration. A summer's day at the beach suggests seashells and blue skies. The early days of autumn signal that it's nearly time to carve a pumpkin—or bake a pumpkin pie. A sudden snowstorm fills the mind's eye with fluffy white mounds and crackling ice crystals. The sudden arrival of daffodils announces the coming of spring. Let these seasonal objects, colors, and ideas be the centerpieces of your layouts, and your scrapbook will soon be filled with lively pages. There's still another advantage to seasonal scrapbooking. At least four times a year, as one season ends and another begins, you'll have extra incentive to get busy making pages.

▶ MAKING A SCARECROW, *(top)* DONNA COMMONS, JACKSONVILLE, FLORIDA

If at first you don't succeed—this artist was so caught up in the moment, she forgot to take the picture! Her accommodating young sons took their scarecrow apart and rebuilt him so she could record the moment in her scrapbook page.

▶ HOLLY, *(bottom)* KELLEY BLONDIN, GRAND BLANC, MICHIGAN

While shopping for supplies, this scrapbook artist spotted a perfect photo opportunity. The outside of the craft store was decorated for fall—so, she seized the moment and set her daughter Holly down for a portrait. The autumnal colors of the quilt block, letter, and pumpkin stickers accent the seasonal theme.

◀ PILES OF SMILES, TRISH TILDEN, WESTMONT, ILLINOIS, AND TINA WEATHERHEAD, WOODRIDGE, ILLINOIS

Tumbling leaves, made from photographs punched with a leaf-shaped punch, surround smiling faces silhouetted against cut brown paper to re-create the playful sense of a joyful jump into the leaves.

▲ AT THE BEACH, Susan Walker, Oakbrook
Terrace, Illinois
....
*Hand-coloring adds soft tints to black-and-white photographs. Stenciled
starfish and seashell shapes are cut out of pastel papers.*

▶ HILTON BEACH, Jenny Lowhar, Miami, Florida
....
*A summertime image of a child contentedly digging in the sand at the
seashore is warm enough to keep the winter chills and blahs at more than
arm's length.*

▶▶ WATER FUN, Charlotte Wilhite, Fort Worth,
Texas
....
*Learning to swim is a milestone in your child's life—and in yours. With the
help of an underwater disposable camera, colored papers, colored pens, a
circle template, and fish stickers, this scrapbook artist recorded her four-
year-old son's adventures under water. The journaling lines are song lyrics
from the Disney film* The Little Mermaid.

▲ THANKSGIVING, Kathy Guier, Downey, California

This scrapbooker created the mottled look of autumn leaves by sponging fall colors onto neutral-colored paper. The leaves were punched and then textured with a paper crimper. Her family's Thanksgiving memories, matted in circle shapes, float like falling leaves around the tree.

▶ PUMPKIN PATCH, Lissa Mitchell, Kansas City, Missouri

This cheerful, seasonal pumpkin was created with a puzzle template—an easy way to frame your photos.

ILLUSION PAGES

1. Enlarge the pattern below to a size that fits your scrapbook page (this hexagonal pattern is from the book *Triad Optical Illusions* by Harry Turner, Dover Publications, 1978). Make a copy of the pattern so you can refer to it as you work.

2. Each of the six blocks is made of three shaded sections. Choose light, medium, and dark papers to work with to show the shading. Cut out the three sections of one of the blocks. Trace each shaded piece onto colored or printed paper that matches the degree of shading. Reassemble the block and tape the pieces in place.

3. Now, choose your photos. Match the shade of each photo with the shade of its mat to add to the three-dimensional effect. Working on a lightbox, trace the pattern over the photograph. Trim the photograph about ¼ inch on all sides and mount it on the mat. Crop and mat each photo—including the center photo.

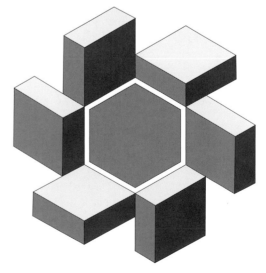

▲ PUMPKIN HARVEST, ARTWORK: CONNIE MIEDEN (COX), WESTMINSTER, COLORADO, PHOTOS: SANDRA ESCOBEDA, MANTECA, CALIFORNIA

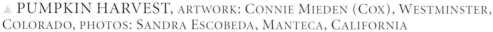

Create the illusion of depth and light with a few tricks of perspective and some simple supplies.

▲ SNOW BOARDERS, KATHLEEN PANEITZ, LONGMONT, COLORADO

....

This delightful winter scene uses accents of vellum perfectly. The icy letters cut from dark blue paper and realistic snowflakes in a dark blue sky are finished with a layer of cut vellum.

◄ SNOWMAN, TerryAnn BENEDICT, BELT, MONTANA

....

A simple, wreath-shaped design made with a circle template makes a playful page of memories for the proud builder of this snowman. The snowman's nose, eyes, and mouth are cut out with deckle-edged scissors, and his cutout top hat completes his classic look.

▶ SNOWY DAYS, DOROTHY FERREIRA, WOODCLIFF LAKE, NEW JERSEY

....

This scrapbook artist is also a quilter, so she made a "warm and cozy quilt" of her pictures of her children's snowy days, juxtaposing photos and illustrations.

SNOWY

Winter 1994 Brought more
snow for us to Play with.
Shelby was big enough
to really enjoy
It all. Jay
would use his
Plow to make big
Piles of snow for the
Kids to make igloos with.

DAYS

► WINTER STREAM, PAMELA ZENGER, SPOKANE, WASHINGTON

....

A line of verse from the Book of Psalms adds to the reflective mood of this quiet winter scene. Die cuts, deckle scissored paper, and small punched snowflakes and leaves accent the black-and-white photo to create the wintry effect.

◄ SNOW, OKSANNA POPE, LOS GATOS, CALIFORNIA

....

Remember that snowy sixth birthday? This sparkling page brightens the photos—and the memory of a wintry day at Lake Tahoe—with a background that echoes the colors and textures of the photographs.

▼ BLAME IT ON EL NIÑO, JEANNE CIOLLI, DOVE CANYON, CALIFORNIA

....

The unexpected thrill of a sudden snowstorm in April made these skiers' day! To make the most of her theme, Jeanne iced her pages with mounds of decorative die-cut snowflakes.

PUNCHED FLOWERS

LARGE FLOWERS: Old tree, medium apple, small heart, ¹/8-inch round hand punch. Punch and assemble as shown. For the softened edge effect, gently roll the edges of the flowers and leaves around a pencil before placing on the page. A medium butterfly punch finished the page.

LILACS: Small heart, diamond mini extension, negative squares from southwest border, ¹/16-inch round hand punch. Punch and assemble as shown.

LARGE FLOWER BUDS: Old tree, medium heart. Punch and assemble as shown.

▲ BUTTERFLIES & BLOOMS, ARTWORK: PAM KLASSEN, WESTMINSTER, COLORADO, PHOTO: ERICIA PIEROVICH, LONGMONT, COLORADO

A portrait photograph and layers of punched lilacs, flowers, and butterflies turn Alexandra's summer of 1998 into a lush, blossom-filled garden.

▶ SPRING PORTRAITS, MARILYN GARNER, SAN DIEGO, CALIFORNIA

Simple presentations sometimes call out for an unusual, decorative touch. These fanciful flowers add a touch of spring when used as borders or frames to such inviting outdoor portraits. Use the folded floral shapes alone or in clusters.

FOLDED FLOWERS

Cut a circle of colored paper with a circle cutter or template (this sample is 2 ¹/₈ inches in diameter). Fold the circle in half, then fold it in half again to form a quarter circle.

Unfold the quarter circle so that the paper is a half circle again. Now fold the outer edge of each quarter circle into the center crease. Fold the edges in again. Now unfold the paper so that it is a full circle. On the back side of the circle, mark and number each crease from 1 to 16, working clockwise, as shown.

To complete the folded flower, follow this sequence of steps: Fold crease 10 to 12. Fold 7 to 9. Fold 4 to 6. Crease the flower at 2 and 13. Layer each folded flower beneath a punched green bell, as shown.

Miss Hannah 1999

THE DRESDAN PLATE

To make your template, draw a circle to fit your page. Then draw another circle within it to the size you want your central photograph to be. Divide the outer circle into sixteen or twenty equal parts. These will form the "fans" of the plate.

1. Using the pattern below, make a template for the segments. Trace the shape onto printed paper.

2. Cut the shapes. For this design, you'll need sixteen pieces.

3. Find and lightly mark the center of your page with a pencil. Draw a 1-inch-diameter circle at the center of the page. Arrange the fans around the small circle, making sure they are aligned.

Crop your photo to the desired size. Add a mat and adhere the photo to the center of the page. Add a title below the photo if you wish.

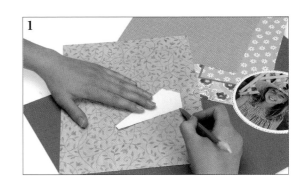

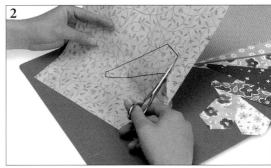

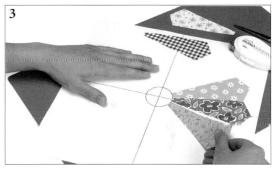

◄ ◄ MISS HANNAH, MARILYN GARNER, SAN DIEGO, CALIFORNIA

This cheerful page features a portrait of Hannah in her sunbonnet, framed by colorful prints arranged in the pattern of a traditional Dresdan Plate quilt pattern, which was popular in the 1930s and 1940s.

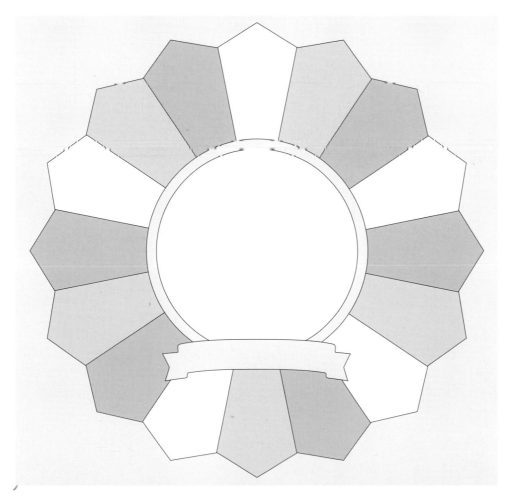

OUR

FAMILY

TRADITIONS

1999

JANUARY

HAVING A VALENTINES
LUNCH WITH MY FRIENDS
FROM COLLEGE.

FEBRUARY

MARCH

APRIL

ANNUAL EASTER EGG HUNT
WITH OUR COUSINS.

JUNE

THE FAMILY REUNION
HELD AT OUR H
THE FOURTH OF

OCTOBER

A BIRTHDAY PHOTO
COMPLETE WITH CAKE
AND BALLOONS.

OUR HAL
ALWAYS
FO

MAY

AT THANKS
TURKEY D

EVERYBODY GETS BREAKFAST
IN BED ON THEIR BIRTHDAY.

SUMMER VACATION IN
CALIFORNIA AT GRANDPA
& GRANDMA'S BEACH HOUSE.

JULY·

SEPTEMBER·

POSING WITH DAD ON THE FIRST DAY OF SCHOOL·

NOVEMBER·

EEN PARTY
UDES BOBBING
PPLES.

DECEMBER

NG WE HAVE A
ER WITH MOM & DAD.

OUR KIDS ARE ALWAYS
PART OF THE CHRISTMAS
PROGRAM AT OUR CHURCH

SHARED MOMENTS, SPECIAL EVENTS

Special family events provide another rich theme around which to organize the pages of your scrapbook. How you define special is up to you. You might want to record your son's first days of school—every year, until the year he graduates from high school. Or you might want to make much of the day that your little girl lost her first tooth or read her first chapter book all by herself. Special sports, academic, or musical achievements—like the home team's winning games or your youngster's violin recital—also make wonderful themes for pages that will bring pride and joy for years to come.

Think about those simple, special events that you and your family share as a group, too. Is there something that you and your family especially like to do together? Pizza and a movie on Friday nights? Canoe trips on the lake every other Sunday? Visits to the zoo once in a while? Whatever the activity is, record it in your scrapbook. Because they are shared, even the simplest moments have a great significance in your family's life.

Of course, family vacations are shared events, too, and they provide myriad themes for your scrapbook pages. Your camera is usually at the ready—and there are plenty of colorful sights, action-packed adventures, and special moments to record. And don't forget to document the road trip, too—sometimes getting there is half the fun!

◄ OUR FAMILY TRADITIONS, ARTWORK: ERIKIA GHUMM, BRIGHTON, COLORADO, PHOTOS: JOYCE FEIL, GOLDEN, COLORADO

Special events happen all year round. See for yourself. Try scrapbook pages that celebrate—in words and pictures—the traditions your family shares each month of the year.

▶ PIZZA NIGHT, ARTWORK: PAM KLASSEN, WESTMINSTER, COLORADO, PHOTOS: PENNIE STUTZMAN, BROOMFIELD, COLORADO

Even the simplest traditions are worth preserving—like Saturday morning breakfasts or Friday pizza nights.

▶▶ BABTSIA'S PASKA, OKSANNA POPE, LOS GATOS, CALIFORNIA

Oksanna scrapbooked about a favorite Ukranian Easter tradition that centers around paska, a special type of bread her mother bakes every year for the event.

▼ SCHOOLBUS CAKE, DEBBIE LAITINEN, SEYMOUR, INDIANA

When Tyler came home from his first day of school, Debbie surprised him with a cake she had baked just for him—in the shape of a schoolbus! She has since celebrated every one of her kids' first day of school the same way.

Easter

is a wonderful time of year
and full of *Tradition*. Our family starts off
by celebrating our Saviour's reserection at church.

During lunch at my Mom's and Dad's we write our names on the cross made out of bread. My mom also shares with family and neighbors special Ukrainin bread named "*paska*."

After dinner we select our eggs for the big *Egg Smashing* contest. You turn to your neighbor to challenge them. There are all sorts of technics and styles; hit slow but hard, strike fast but low etc... The winner gets to keep the other persons egg and moves on to the next victim.

Whatever you want to call it it's wonderful and in our Baba's and Dido's house it's tradition at Easter.

HOW TO PRESERVE TRADITIONS

Traditions do not have to be complex rituals passed down from your ancestors. Many families create traditions of their own: movie nights, special birthday breakfasts, annual photos on the front porch. No matter the size or significance of your traditions, include them in your scrapbook. Here are some hints for preserving them:

Photograph elements of your tradition at least once—special food, activities, preparations?

• JOURNAL. The only way to pass on the reason behind the tradition is through words. Write down the origin of the tradition. When did it begin and why? Don't feel obligated to pen lengthy paragraphs; bulleted information works just as well.

• INCLUDE PEOPLE. What role does each family member play in the tradition? Even if it's just as the movie-picker-outer for family movie night or the babysitter for your weekly date night, include each person's photo and journal about his or her role.

• INCORPORATE COLORS. If specific colors are significant in the tradition, use them in the page design. There are traditional colors—red and green for Christmas, blue or silver at Hanukkah—or your family might have special colors to wear each year for family photos. Make a frame or background using the colors and journal about their significance.

• HIGHLIGHT SYMBOLS. Photograph or enlarge symbols closely associated with your traditions. Remember to include a description of their meaning if you know it.

• TALK TO OLDER RELATIVES. If the tradition is an old one, and the significance is unknown, interview older family members to find out if they know the origin. Include memories of traditions by younger members as well.

▼ SATURDAY MORNINGS, MICHELE GERBRANDT,
WESTMINSTER, COLORADO

*Traditions don't always revolve around the holidays. Our daily routines and spe-
cial weekly events also make wonderful memories. Every Saturday morning, I
make fresh popovers for my family–just like my mom always did. I never
thought of this routine as a "family tradition," until my husband called it one.
So, I created a pop-up popover page for my scrapbook–featuring my daughter
Anna, who is carrying on the tradition by learning to make popovers, too!*

EVERY SATURDAY MORNING POPOVERS

① SET OVEN TO 400°

② GREASE MUFFIN PAN

③ GATHER INGREDIENTS

④ MIX TOGETHER

POP-UP PAGES

For a lively layout, make your pages jump up and out, pop-up, or peek-a-boo. Choose a pop-up feature that matches your theme.

1. Copy the pop-up template on page 140, or draw your own to fit your album. Fold the template along the center fold line. Fold the tabs up along the fold line.

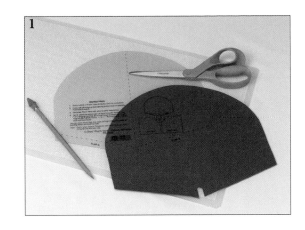

2. Crop your photograph to the shape of the pop-up. For these pages, the popover was drawn freehand, cut as a separate piece, and attached to the back of the photograph. Fold the photograph and the popover along the pop-up fold lines. Fold the bottom edges along the tab folds.

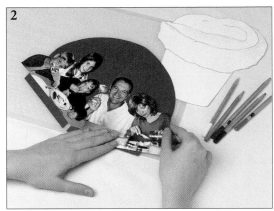

3. Fold the pop-up along the center fold line. Fold tabs up along the bottom edge. Measure the gap between the pages in the album you are using. Position the left and right pages so that the center gap is the same width. It's important that each side of the pop-up stand is positioned in the exact location on opposite pages.

To accomplish this, make sure the notched end of the base is approximately 3 inches down from the upper edge of the page. Then angle out so the opposite ends of the base fall approximately 2 to 3 inches away from the gutter at the upper edge of the page. Pencil mark this location, then adhere the pop-up to your page. When you close the album, the stand should fold neatly to the interior of the two-page spread.

TIP

For extra dimension and detail, decorate your pop-up with die cuts, punched shapes, colored drawings, and journaling.

*At last they meet! Grandpa Gerbrandt traveled from
California to Colorado to meet his new great-grandson,
Daniel. Of his fourteen great-grandchildren, only two of the
boys share his name. This portrait shows the four generations
of fathers and sons who carry on the Gerbrandt family name:
Daniel, his father Ron, his grandfather Gordon, and, of course,
his great-grandfather Abe.*

*Solid and patterned printed paper mats, stickers aplenty, die-
cut frames, intriguingly cut photos, frames, and mats all contribute to a vibrant and fun-filled picture of contemporary
family life from holidays and vacations to everyday moments.*

FOUR GENERATIONS, Twyla Stair, Lubbock, Texas

Lauren and Meredith love to spend time with Great Granny on her farm. Patterned papers in gingham and plaid add a homey touch to these generation pages made for the girls by their mother, Twyla. The ribbons are cut freehand. The bows are made with a template. Both are boldly outlined and detailed with a thick black pen. The journaling is done with a more delicate line.

GRANDMA'S GIFT TO AMY, Artwork: Pam Klassen, Westminster, Colorado

A simple presentation is as effective as a more elaborate one when the moment speaks for itself. A devoted grandma who knows just what is on the mind of her second youngest grandchild has a special gift for the little girl on the occasion of her baby sister's christening. The candid photograph is simply cropped and presented on a background of punched pastel printed papers beneath a layer of soft vellum—a lovely way to remember a tender moment on a special family day.

SISTERS IN SPIRIT

MACKENZIE 3 YRS. OLD

XIAO
3

ADOPTION DAY.

ELEVEN LITTLE GIRLS WERE ADOPTED FROM CHINA ON THE SAME DAY. ALTHOUGH THEY LIVE FAR APART, THEIR PARENTS HELP THEM REMAIN CONNECTED BY GETTING TOGETHER ONCE A YEAR.

A REUNION 3 YEARS LATER. GIRLS SETTING IN SAME ORDER.

JULIA
3 YRS. OLD

A MAP OF A JOURNEY
of love and faith—led by God,
traveled by Lindsay and Peter to
find Xiaoling and bring her home to
her place in the family, now complete.

SISTERS IN SPIRIT

Every year, eleven little Chinese girls—who were all adopted on the same day—travel from all over the United States to gather together again. These "sisters in spirit" spend the day playing, while forging a special bond that will last a lifetime. The photographs at left show the infants in a row on adoption day in Guangzhou, China, and then, three years later, as toddlers, seated in the same order in the U. S. —*Artwork: Erikia Ghumm, Brighton, Colorado, photos: Jamie Kilmartin*

▲ **A BOOK ABOUT ME**, ARTWORK: PAM KLASSEN, WESTMINSTER, COLORADO, PHOTO: LORALEE DISCHNER, DENVER, COLORADO

For writers, there's an old saying, "Write about what you know best." For scrapbookers, it's not much different. Sometimes the best place to start your family story is with yourself!

GRADUATED PAGES

To create these pages, you'll need a spiral-bound album. Place wavy stickers along the edges of the second page in the album. Allow the stickers to overlap at the corners. With a straight-edged ruler and a craft knife, miter the corners of the intersecting stickers to form a clean angle. Cut away the excess strips of the stickers.

Now, with scissors, trim the page close to the edges of the border stickers. Next, measure the distance from the page's edge to the inside of the sticker. Trim the first page of the album to that measurement—so that its edge will align with the inside edge of the border sticker on the second page.

If you want to add a colored vellum insert, cut the vellum to the size of the album. Lay the paper next to the spiral binding. With pencil, mark the location of the spirals on the vellum. Now punch over the marks with a square punch. Make slits from the edge of the paper into the punched spaces. Insert the vellum sheet behind the second, wavy-bordered page.

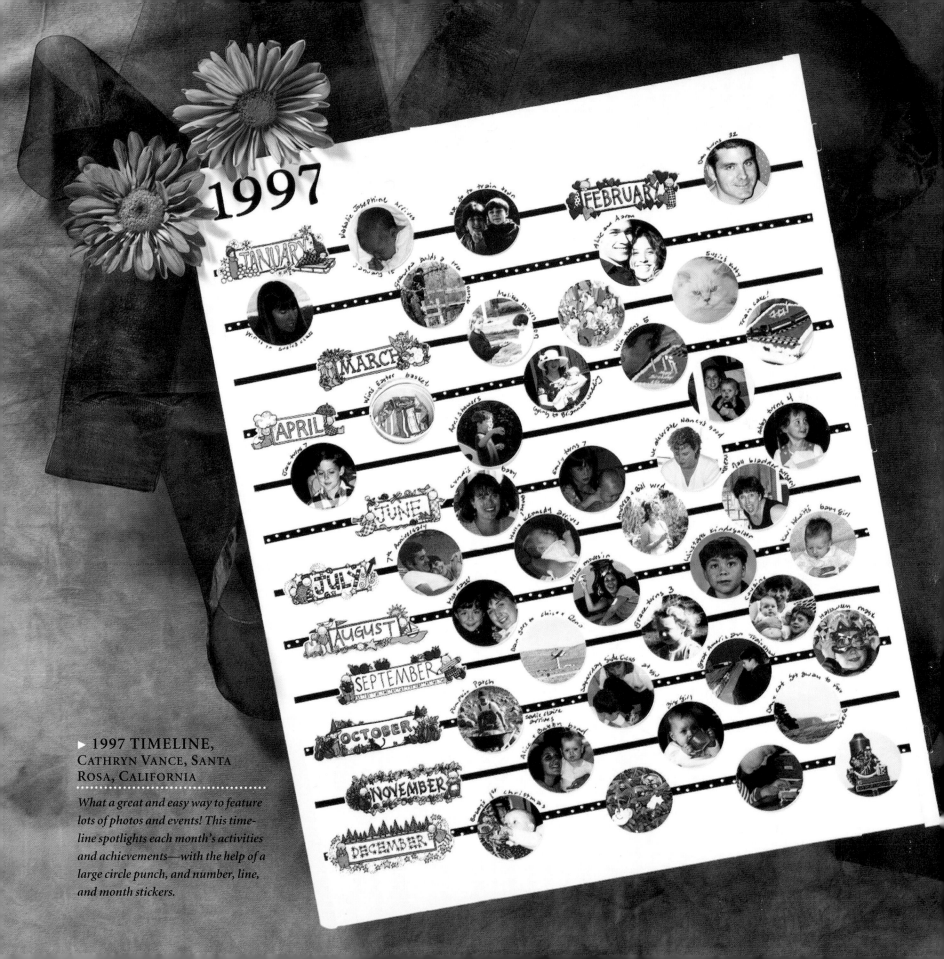

▶ 1997 TIMELINE,
CATHRYN VANCE, SANTA
ROSA, CALIFORNIA

*What a great and easy way to feature
lots of photos and events! This timeline spotlights each month's activities
and achievements—with the help of a
large circle punch, and number, line,
and month stickers.*

▶ HAPPY HEARTS, Teresa Villanueva, Aurora, Colorado

With colored-paper appliqués and drawn "stitch" lines, this simple quilt page presents four cheerful portraits.

◀ HUGS & KISSES, Charla Campbell, Springfield, Missouri

This Valentine's Day page features two portraits, simply sweetened by the accents of bright red against the neutral black-and-white color scheme. The roses in the photos were cut from color prints of the same scenes and positioned in exactly the same places on the black-and-white prints. The photos sit on a lacy mat cut with decorative-edged scissors and detailed with drawn black lines. The matted photos sit on a deep red, textured paper with soft, feathery edges. Cut-out hearts on white mats trimmed with scallop scissors hold the hand-lettering for the title. Punched and layered circles form the roses that are scattered on the "ground."

▲ ST. MARGARET'S SCHOOL, ARTWORK: ERIKIA GHUMM, BRIGHTON, COLORADO, PHOTOS: TRACY KOZLOWSKI, SAN CLEMENTE, CALIFORNIA

Tracy made an appreciation album for her son's preschool teacher. The brightly colored schoolhouse has fold-open doors and windows that reveal photographs of the whole gang.

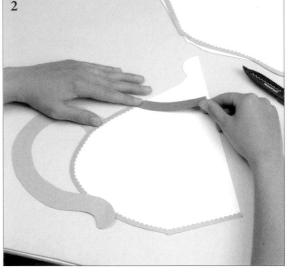

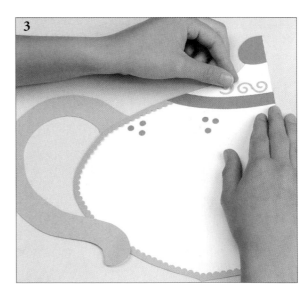

TEAPOT CUT-OUT PAGES

Here's a clever way to get lots of photos and birthday cards into just a few pages. Make the teapot pages first, then place them into the scrapbook pages.

1. Working with the template on page 140, cut out the teapot halves from white scrapbook pages. Center the page hinges.

2. With scallop scissors, cut pink strips as a border for the edges of the teapot. Cut pink handles and curved blue strips and circles for the lid.

3. Punch and arrange small pink swirls to decorate the lid. Punch ¼-inch blue circles to decorate the pot. When you have attached the teapot to the pages, crop and mat the photos. Journal with pink pens and add punched flowers and stickers as accents. To make the page borders, cut blue and white strips with a scalloped ruler. Punch ⅛-inch holes in the white strips. Lay the blue strips along each page edge. Lay the white strips over the blue strips. Draw black dots and dashes to connect the holes.

Chinese Tea Ceremony

One of the most important part of a wedding for Chinese people is the tea ceremony. This is the time when the marriage of the couple is truly acknowledged by Chinese families. Because this was a tradition for my family, the tea ceremony was performed at my parents' house. Our entire family got together and dim sum & other goodies were set out for the feast. After I put on my red silk gown & red satin shoes, I hid and waited for my groom to come and get me. My grandma stayed with me to protect me. While we are all waiting for him to come. Since I am the eldest daughter, this was a very special time for our family.

9.27.98

KNOCK KNOCK
KNOCK KNOCK
KNOCK KNOCK!

Randall had to wait quite some time before Judy would even answer the door. Then, he had to bribe Judy, Bonnie, Elbert, & Gail with red envelopes so they would let him in.

Coming In !

▲ CHINESE TEA CEREMONY,
WENDY FONG, ALEMEDA,
CALIFORNIA

Wendy's scrapbook records and celebrates the many special events that took place as part of her wedding celebration. Each page also celebrates her family heritage and traditions. On these pages, Wendy's journaling describes the importance of the tea ceremony in a Chinese wedding. The ancient traditions come to life in the present day with photographs and fond anecdotes about family and friends who shared the special ceremony, which took place in her parents' home.

◀ BIRTHDAY TEA PARTY,
SHAWN GLAHN, TEMECULA,
CALIFORNIA

In years to come, these girls will certainly cherish these lovely pages of their backyard tea party. The pastel colors, the teapot cutout, and the flowery page details perfectly portray the festive events of the day.

CHINESE TEA CEREMONY

The first thing Wendy Fong thought about when she became engaged was preserving every detail of her wedding, from traditional Chinese ceremonies to reception seating charts. She created two scrapbooks for the project describing the traditions in her journaling so their significance will never be lost. She could remember many images—including a roasted pig, lots of sweet cakes, and cups of steaming tea, but they were all jumbled and she wasn't sure of their meaning. Grandmother's advice was sought to help Wendy do everything in the traditional Chinese way. One of the most important parts of a wedding for Chinese people is the tea ceremony, during which the couple is truly acknowledged by the Chinese families. The bride, dressed in a traditional Chinese red dress, hides in her family home to wait for the groom to come and get her. Not only does the groom have to find his bride, he has to bribe family members with bright red envelopes to let him into the house. The ceremony is light-hearted and fun, and is finished off with a feast of dim sum and "other goodies."—*Wendy Fong, Alameda, California*

Family outings provide the perfect subjects for scrapbook pages. To make the shapes that set off this jungle theme, Maggie worked with nature stamps that she had purchased to decorate her bathroom walls.

LAYERED STAMPING

To create the patterned background, apply ink to a swirl-shaped stamp. Tap the excess ink onto scrap paper. Randomly stamp swirls onto the background sheet.

Stamp other designs in colors of your choice. This scrapbooker stamped leaves in light blue and gray-green, flowers in magenta and salmon, swirls in blue and medium gray. Make as many designs as you'll need to frame the photos on your page.

Now cut out each shape, leaving a narrow solid border around the design.

To add more texture, punch 1/16-inch holes with a hand punch in the stamped cutouts before you mount them on the page.

▲ GREAT RENO BALLOON RACE, Elisa Purnell, Camarillo, California

These pages record the color and excitement of the hot-air balloon race itself. The photographs were cut with a diamond-shaped template and pieced together mosaic-style. The pattern makes a great design, and more photos can fit on the pages, too.

THE HOLIDAYS

As families gather around the Thanksgiving table or Christmas tree, light the Menorah, or carve the pumpkin, they are sharing the same traditions that most of us share. The holiday memories that each family creates, however, are uniquely its own. Each family has its own rituals and special observances—certain table linens that are always used, cakes that are always baked, songs that are always sung. There's no better time than the holidays to catch a glimpse of just what gives your family its special identity.

So, take out your camera—and your scrapbooking supplies. Relatives who live at a distance and don't visit often are likely to travel far to attend these festive, yearly gatherings. Your lens will find the family resemblances, capture the candid moments that deepen relationships, and record the traditional foods and activities that your family looks forward to so eagerly each year—perhaps the same kinds of food and activities your ancestors enjoyed in another land years ago.

If there are children in the family, you and your camera will no doubt seek them out. Children are the heart of the holidays. Portraits of youngsters on Santa's knee or wide-eyed around packages on Christmas Eve capture the very essence of the holiday. You can tell the story with a simple portrait matted with red and green or with an elaborately decorated page with a festooned pop-up Christmas tree. The choice is yours, and the possibilities are endless. You might decide to give thanks for your bounty of family and friends in a cornucopia filled with photographs of the Thanksgiving Day feast. Or you may decide to make a practical holiday page that literally holds a "pocketful" of Happy Hanukkah memories. And don't overlook those little holidays—the Fourth of July, Halloween, and, of course, Valentine's Day. Have fun arranging stars and stripes, pumpkins and spiders, and hearts and arrows as you design festive pages with style and memories that are all your own.

▲ BIRTHDAY CAKES, *(top)* CATHIE ALLAN, EDMONTON, ALBERTA, CANADA

Papa's birthday page features the guest of honor—the little girl whose scrapbook page this will someday be. A selective palette of shades of blue and turquoise plus a mustard yellow decorates the cheerful page with double mats, swirling die-cuts, and ornamental type. Balloons contain the basic journaling.

◄ RADIANT STAR QUILT, *(bottom)* RITA BREI, MISSION VIEJO, CALIFORNIA

This page design is based on the Feathered Star, a quilt block from the nineteenth century. The scrapbooker framed her modern photos with this traditional pattern to make a page that spans generations. In a scrapbook made for her children, this page records their grandmother's summer birthday party.

▲ FAMILY PORTRAITS, MARGI BONTRAGER,
KOKOMO, INDIANA

. . . .

*Even a few moments spent outdoors can be the inspiration for beautiful
family pages. The natural setting of Florida is perfect for these flattering
portraits. The cascading tree branches in the photographs inspired the
scrapbooker to create a similar design on the pages themselves with
punched and cut leaves.*

▶ TRICK OR TREAT, ILSA SCHRENK, TALLAHASSEE,
FLORIDA

. . . .

*Bold graphic design sets off this fun-loving Halloween night celebration
page. Orange mats leap off the black background. The black title squares,
matted with orange, each holdand individual letter each one of which is
created with a white pen or seasonal stickers. Photos and mats are
cropped with pinking scissors and corner rounder. The fence, cat, and
witch are all stickers.*

Thanksgiving

Our Bountiful

▲ SPIDER WEB, Donna Pittard, Kingwood, Texas

Have fun with the holidays! Let your imagination run a little wild—and your pages will become extra special. On the page shown above, journaling and a special spider-web effect make the most of the memory of a two-year-old's first Halloween. The web was cut in one piece from white paper with a craft knife and mat. The photos were cropped to fit the spaces in the web. The background is black paper with a border of woodgrain paper strips.

◄ OUR BOUNTIFUL HARVEST, Donna Pittard, Kingwood, Texas

Every occasion has special symbols or traditional motifs. Make the most of them! The bounty and blessings of family are captured in this scrapbook artist's Thanksgiving Day horn of plenty. The photographs of three generations of family are cropped and matted on the fruit and vegetable shapes that spill out of the cornucopia. The photos were cropped to be slightly smaller than the autumn-colored mats. The grapes were punched from small and medium circle punches. The horn and ribbon were shaded with colored pencils and chalk. Fine details and the title lettering were drawn with colored pen.

▲ HAPPY HANUKKAH, ILESE SCHRENK, TALLAHASSEE, FLORIDA

A pocket folder in this page holds holiday cards to preserve the greetings of family and friends. The background is a printed paper. The pocket is cut from a gold sheet and cut with deckle-edged scissors. The postage stamp and the photographs are also cut with deckle edges. Colorful Menorah stickers and journaling in white pen finish the page.

▶ HAPPY HANUKKAH, LORIE SAVINAR, DENVER, COLORADO

The gift-giving traditions of Hanukkah inspired the simple design of this scrapbooker's holiday pages. Wallet-sized photographs of her toddler, Lorie, fit perfectly in gift boxes "tied" with bows of blue and silver metallic papers. The gift box and bow shapes are made with die cuts. The white lettering of the title was drawn with a letter template and silver pen.

hanukkah

19 99

◀ **SWADDLED BABES,** CHARLA CAMPBELL, SPRINGFIELD, MISSOURI

Inspired by baby photographer Anne Geddes, this scrapbooker modeled her daughter Kayla in swaddling clothes and gingerbread and snowman costumes. The design of each page echoes the mood, theme, colors, and textures of the photograph.

PAPER PIECING

1. Place the poinsettia stencil on the scrapbook page so that the design is right side up. Now, turn the stencil over on a flat surface. Place colored paper on top of the stencil. Outline each shape with an embossing stylus. For light papers, work on a light table. For dark papers, emboss by feel, lifting the paper to check your work as needed.

2. Cut out each embossed shape just outside the raised area.

3. Arrange the poinsettia pieces in the corners of the layout, with the embossed surfaces face up. This page was made using a commercially available stencil.

▲ POINSETTIAS, SUSAN WALKER, OAKBROOK TERRACE, ILLINOIS

Embossed petals, leaves, and ribbons brighten the festive mood of these Christmas Eve memories. A simple poinsettia motif and bold color scheme create a powerful frame for candid photos of gift-sharing scenes.

The scrapbook page contains handwritten journaling (ABC format) with the following readable text:

need to worry about travelling too much on the icy streets. Julie & Dan's home is so cozy and welcoming - and hugs and kisses were plentiful - even with dogs Lou and Titi. Lots of phone calls relaying affectionate Christmas greetings were placed to extended family members and close friends - especially to Mère - to tell her how much we missed and loved her. After a late evening of high-tech multi-participant video games, front porch cigar smoking(!), and silliness, and with cinnamon "monkey bread" and Nancy's cheese/bacon/spinach casserole ready for early morning baking, everyone headed upstairs for a short winter's nap. Opening stocking presents is never a quiet affair in our family! It wasn't long before mounds of shiny paper mingled with the fun and thoughtful gifts on the den table. Even family mascot, Flo the flamingo joined the fun attired in her santa hat. But when Père read Mère's touching 'in absentia' greeting to us, Redmond seemed like a long...

CHRISTMAS in Redmond

1998

▲ CHRISTMAS ABCS, NANCY WAGNER, LAGUNA BEACH, CALIFORNIA

After losing all her family photos in a house fire, this artist turned to scrapbooking as "a way to tangibly rebuild the past." In these wonderful and whimsical pages, she uses journaling to capture the events and the feeling of Christmas with her family. "Our family together time," she writes, is what makes the day special. She knows that "our memories will last a lifetime—and beyond (if Nancy's scrapbooking does its job)."

◄ DEAR SANTA, TERRI ROBICHON, PLYMOUTH, MINNESOTA

Children are at the heart of Christmas, and captured moments with Santa make the perfect scrapbook pages. Add a playful touch with primary colors, cut-out crayons, and lettering by whichever youngster has mastered his letters—and you have saved beautiful memories in no time at all!

▼ CHRISTMAS MEMORIES, DONNA PITTARD, KINGWOOD, TEXAS

This festive holiday banner contains lots of journaling about a special Christmas shared by three generations of the Pittard family.

► HAPPY NEW
MILLENNIUM 2000,
CHARLA CAMPBELL,
SPRINGFIELD,
MISSOURI
....

*Where were you when the
new century began? This
scrapbook page records
history for these three children who will someday say,
"I was there."*

▲ WEDDING PORTRAIT, Kristen Mason, Reston, Virginia

This scrapbook title page features a simple frame made of die-cut hearts and doves. Pierced edges add texture to the die cuts. The colors and design of the border convey the mood and style of this couple's special day.

▲ LISA AND DOUGLAS, Pat Murray, Edmonton, Alberta, Canada

Pressed flowers from the bride's bouquet add a special touch to this wedding portrait. Flower stickers extend the theme. Enclose pressed flowers and memorabilia in self-adhesive pockets or slip the page into a page protector.

WEDDINGS AND FORMAL EVENTS

As they do for the big holidays, families also gather together for other types of special events—weddings, christenings, silver or golden anniversaries, for example. These kinds of gatherings are slightly different from holiday gatherings, however. These gatherings have superstars! The couple or the baby at the center of the event is without a doubt the main attraction.

Design your scrapbook pages to reflect that star status. When considering your layout, think about where you will focus attention on the page. Adjust the sizes and placement of images to direct the viewer's eye to the person or people being honored. The portrait of the subject should be the centerpiece of the layout—even if there are photographs of other people on the page, as in the folded-flap wedding page opposite.

Formal occasions usually suggest elegant and sophisticated page designs. Try working with quiet colors and simple motifs, as in the white die-cut heart and dove border shown above left. Add whatever decorative elements best mirror the mood of the event you wish to portray—pressed flowers, memorabilia in protective boxes, silky or lacy fabrics, delicately patterned papers or vellum sheets. Your journaling about the setting, the people, and your own thoughts and feelings will provide an extra layer of meaning. Decorative lettering in special metallic or colored inks add an impressive finishing touch to your page.

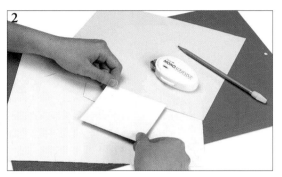

▲ WEDDING DOORS, Pam Metzger, Boulder, Colorado

Add an extra layer of journaling and photographs to your pages by adding "doors" and "windows" that open.

TRADITIONAL WEDDING ALBUM

In this heirloom scrapbook, the special moments of a couple's wedding day are showcased in a honeycomb pattern. Five rows of hexagons, cut from pastel patterned papers, were adhered to a solid cream background sheet. Some of the hexagons frame photographs cut to the same shape. Five of the patterned "doors" hinge open to reveal more smiles and stories inside!

1. Cut a honeycomb of photographs and printed papers with a hexagon-shaped template. Adhere them to a light-colored, solid sheet. Decide which hexagons you want to open, and carefully cut around five sides of each with a craft knife, using a ruler as a guide. The uncut side will be the "door" hinge.

2. Mount a photograph or a soft plain or patterned paper square on the reverse side of the solid sheet, behind each cut door.

3. Add journaling as desired in the blank areas behind hexagon doors.

> **TIP**
>
> When using a template to crop photos, move it around on the photo to determine the best position. Lightly mark cutting lines with the small end of an embossing tool.

Chloe
Jan 18, 1998

Winter coat and hat made
with love by Grammy

▲ WEDDING RING, Caroline Lebel, Toronto, Ontario, Canada

....

Many lovely moments of a spring wedding day are captured on these elegant pages. The candid photographs are integrated into the double-ring quilt pattern and are framed by paper hydrangeas, which are cut to fit the long oval shapes.

◀ CHLOE, Joann Colledge, North Ogden, Utah

....

Grandmother's gift of a handmade coat and hat are the special treasures featured on Chloe's page. The grapevine that frames Chloe's portrait travels around the page, too, in a border of punched maple leaves and 1/8-inch round shapes.

┌───┐

TIP

....

When hunting for scrapbooking supplies, be sure to search for papers and fabrics with interesting patterns and textures. Paper doilies, colored tissues, handmade paper, lace napkins, origami papers, crinoline, calico, satins, and velvets— these, and more, add special spark and sparkle to your scrapbook pages.

└───┘

▲ OUR RINGBEARER, Erin Crawford, San Leandro, California

....

Erin has always wanted to quilt. Here, she has worked patterned papers and punched-paper hearts, daisies, leaves, and suns into a Dresdan Rose quilt pattern.

◄ MICHAEL'S HOLIDAY, Susan
Cobb for Hot Off The Press
· ·
*Michael's holiday visit with Grandma is pre-
served in this delicate page. The photograph is
simply tucked into a colored-vellum pocket,
which has been layered on a lighter vellum
background.*

► FRIENDS AND FAMILY, Pam
Klassen, Westminster, Colorado
· ·
*The French door–style layout makes the most of
this page of family photos. The soft and elegant
vellum "window panes" create a nostalgic holiday mood.*

WORKING WITH VELLUM
· ·
Vellum papers add a unique touch to any album page. Because it is transparent, vellum can change the look of solid and patterned papers, but glues, smudges, and creases are also more likely to show. Here are a few simple tricks for working with vellum to create an endless array of special effects.

If you are layering vellum over other papers, choose papers with bright colors and strong patterns so that the colors and patterns will show through. White vellum softens colors or patterns too bold for your page, colored vellum creates additional special effects. Cut vellum only with pattern-edged scissors that have a small pattern. Creases in vellum paper leave white "scars" on the surface.

Ink does not absorb into vellum as quickly as it does into other papers. When journaling on vellum, be sure to let the ink dry for a few minutes before continuing to work with it. For special effects, color on the reverse side of a sheet of vellum with chalk, markers, or colored pencils. The chalk and colored pencils create a soft, muted look; markers will create a stained-glass effect. Because vellum is transparent, it is also perfect for tracing. A "pocket" made of vellum can be a delicate, sheer way to mount a special photo on a page.

Adhesives also don't absorb into the paper as quickly as they do into other types of paper. If you can, work with photo mounts rather than liquid adhesives. Apply all types of adhesives sparingly directly to the matching surface instead of to the vellum. If any glue shows through the vellum sheet, cover the spot with the punched pieces, die cuts, stickers, or drawings.

Hailey
Garcia

La Mirada
pumpkin patch
1999

Little
Pumpkin

Tomorrow: Turning a New Page

······ ◆ ······

One of the greatest gifts that we can give our children is a strong sense of themselves—a sense of who they are, where they came from, and what they hope to become. With this solid self-confidence, they have a better understanding of their place in the world as they make their way through their lives.

Carefully and lovingly made, with an eye toward the future, your family scrapbook will help provide your children with this solid ground. It will also teach them to appreciate and value their ties to their family and heritage. Through your scrapbook, you can share with young family members the long story of your family's shared affection, special achievements, quirks, and fine qualities. The pages of your scrapbook will tell the stories of centuries and trace the smiling faces of generations of loved ones—many of whom often bear a striking resemblance to each other!

Now, add your newcomer's story to the tale. Record the days long before he was a twinkle in your eye and the happy moment when he arrived in the world. Capture her first words, his play time with best friends, her favorite toys, books, and silly expressions. Mix in your own thoughts, hopes, and dreams, and you'll make the pages even more meaningful. Remember, your scrapbook is a personal statement, made with your own hands and creative energy, love, and affection—all of which become part of the gift that you pass along.

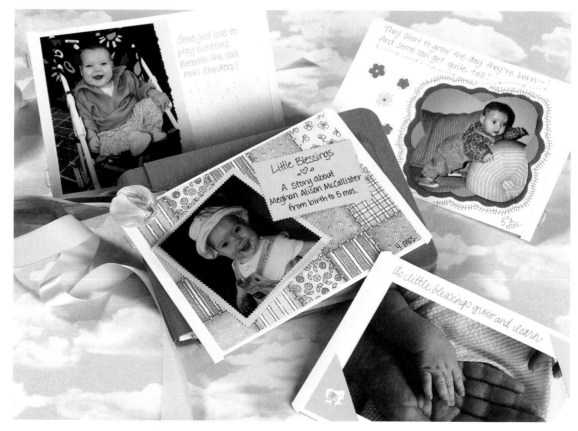

◀ LITTLE PUMPKIN, Sandy Holly, Laguna Hills, California

Seasons come and go quickly as children grow. Record memories by combining colors, shapes, and textures that recall special days. Here, cut autumn leaves of vellum from templates of varying sizes are pierced at the edges, and layered to create a feathery effect. The cut-out paper pumpkin at bottom right seems to be tumbling out of the photo, adding a bright accent to the page.

▲ LITTLE BLESSINGS STORYBOOK ALBUM, Melissa McCallister, Gainesville, Florida

Melissa made four "Little Blessings" books about her daughter, Meghan, as Christmas gifts for Meghan's grandparents and great-grandparents—so they could share the joys of Meghan's first five months of life.

Your family scrapbook will be a source of great joy not only for you, but also for the people you love—a cherished possession that you all turn to again and again. It is a precious heirloom that you will proudly hand down to your children and grandchildren—some who are perhaps still infants, some not yet born. Soon, they will be adding pages and memories of their own—as your family's story continues to unfold through their lifetimes, and beyond.

WELCOME!

When newborns enter our lives, they change everything. After nine months of patient waiting, when time seems to stand still, there is suddenly lots of activity, lots of visitors, and lots of new emotions and discoveries. The pages of your scrapbook will quickly fill with photographs, journaling, and colorful designs that convey the contagious sense of excitement that everyone feels when a new life begins. You'll also want to keep track of baby's first gifts, cards and letters of congratulation, and first experiences—bath time, feedings, and the first smile. The first days and months of a baby's life bustle with rapid growth and miraculous changes. Your scrapbook pages will let you share these thrilling moments with loved ones who live at a distance, but don't want to miss a thing. Design your pages so they retell the story of these extraordinary, fleeting moments—capture the lively playtime activities and the sleepy, quiet moments, too.

▶ SLUMBER SOFTLY LITTLE ONE,
ARTWORK: PAM KLASSEN, WESTMINSTER, COLORADO,
PHOTO: DIANE PERRY, BROOMFIELD, COLORADO

Stamped and heat-embossed stars, sun, and moon fill the skies of this dreamy scene. The sides and lower edges of the cut cloud paper are adhered to the backing, and the top edge is left open as a pocket.

Something for Baby

Awaken gently with the sun & hear the songbirds sing.

...on & Stars

3 months

SweetDreams

John
Michael

3 weeks
old

November
29
1997

Your baby is the newest link in the chain of your family's deep-rooted and continuing story. Welcome the child by adding his or her own pages to your family album. You will be giving your child a great gift. Your pages will record a significant time in his life that he won't be able to remember. Your pages will also show your child, in years to come, how much she was loved and cared for—and what a central role she played in the family, even then.

◄ SWEET DREAMS, MELISA THORNTON, MUNFORD, TENNESSEE

Tender lullabies, splashing baths, first smiles—and even first sniffles and tears. Record all of your growing baby's everyday memories. The years pass quickly, and soon even the simplest, fitful moment will become a precious memory.

▲ INTRODUCING JACK BAYLESS, KATY BAYLESS, ALHAMBRA, CALIFORNIA

Katy designed her page announcing the arrival of the newest member of her family around the theme of a growing garden. "Children are like seeds, in each there is a promise of the future," she wrote in her journaling. To add a realistic touch, the lettering resembles the printing on a seed packet.

◄ I THINK THAT I SHALL NEVER SEE, MARYJO REGIER, LITTLETON, COLORADO

Old and new photos combine with an old illustration of a ship to link past and present on this page. The portrait at center is the grandfather of these little sailors. His ancestors voyaged from Russia to America in 1879—and more than 100 years later, his four grandsons were born here. This one page tells a century of family history.

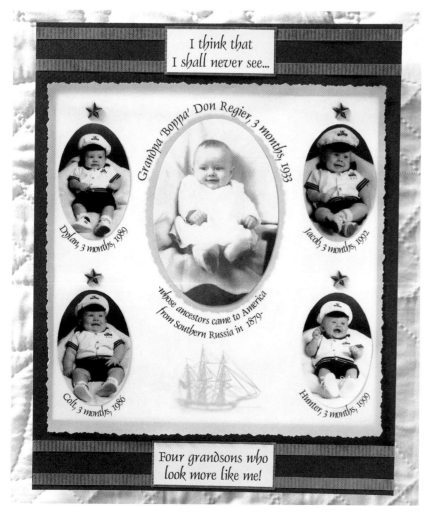

▲ GRANDMOTHER'S FLOWER GARDEN, Sally
Swift, Jacksonville, Florida

▲ EMILY, Jennifer Borowski, Princeton,
New Jersey

Sally "stitches" all of her quilts with a black pen. The many variations of patterned paper now available have made creating quilted scrapbook pages more fun, and even more meaningful to avid scrapbookers like Sally.

This simple page shows the many moods of Emily. The paper-pieced bunny at the top of the page is adapted from the design on her outfit. The "stitch" lines are drawn with pen.

LINKS TO THE PAST

Whenever you have the opportunity, scrapbook in words and pictures to record the relationships of your newborn and other family members. Big brothers, little sisters, aunts, and uncles will all play an important part in your newcomer's life. Those relationships begin the day that the baby arrives. Candid photographs of first meetings or touching moments will make beautiful scrapbook pages. Add some journaling, too—gift-card poems or messages, stories or bits of information about the life of the adult relative. Include a few of your own hopes and dreams for your baby's future, too.

Records of the first meetings or special bonds between grandparents (or great-grandparents!) and the newborn are important documents, full of emotion and special value. As the older members of your family age, recording the times you share becomes more and more important. A new baby in the family certainly gives you the chance to scrapbook about a meaningful and happy event. More important, it gives you the chance to scrapbook about the great and rare opportunity that these generations—sometimes separated in time by almost a hundred years—have to meet and know each other.

Your child has been born into a personal universe that is filled with stories, traditions, and lots of love. Your child's story stretches back in time, just as, with this new life, your family's story now continues to move forward into the future. Your scrapbook pages can be the bridge.

EMILY'S HEIRLOOM QUILT

Six months before Emily Rose Stevenson was born, her grandmother, Marjorie Mann, and her aunt, Janet van Trueren, began making her a very special quilt. The quilt combined old and new fabrics, including pieces from the baby's great-great-grandmother, pearl beads from her mother's bridal veil, and swatches from her mother's childhood clothing. The quilt was presented to Emily on her first birthday and hangs on her bedroom wall. Emily's mother, Tammy, added these pages to Emily's scrapbook to remind her daughter how much she is dearly loved. She photographed each of the quilt blocks and "pieced" them with paper pieces. Her journaling page tells the story of this beautiful gift.
—*Tammy Stevenson, Florissant, Missouri*

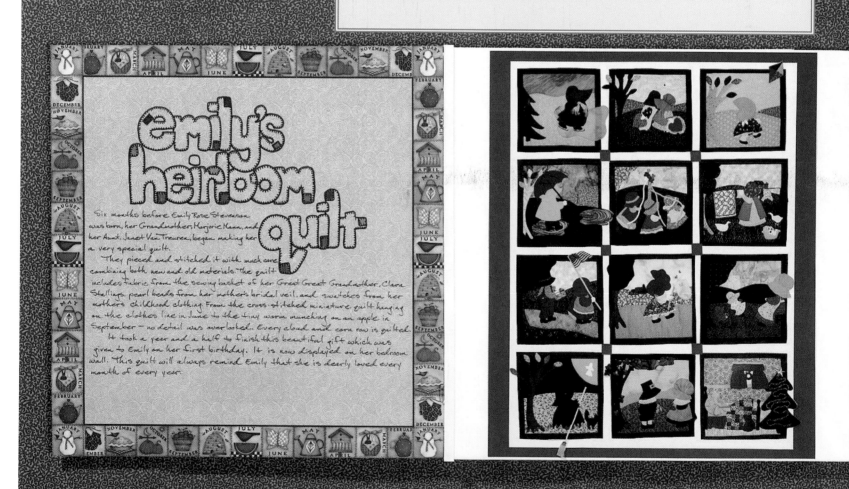

▲ **HUG ME 1ST, 2ND, 3RD AND 4TH!**, Linda
Strauss, Provo, Utah, photos: Tricia Kelly,
Thousand Oaks, California

Stamped babies and tiny ribbons are tucked in the memorabilia holder—
placeholders for future locks of hair from each of the four Kelly quadruplets.

▶ **IT'S THE LITTLE THINGS**, Wendy McKeehan
for Puzzlemates

This delicately patterned album cover announces the stars of the pages
inside this lovely scrapbook. Photographs and journaling of everyday life
will tell the story of Mommy and Tori as they get to know each other.

It's The Little Things

Mommy & Tori 1999

Children are the heart of the family

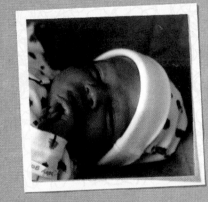

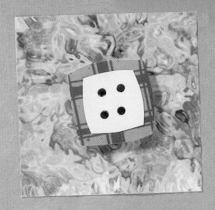

Mommy
Daddy
and
Sawyer
1998

What says it better than these patchwork-style pages? Layers of patterned-paper scraps and punched paper, foam-mounted "buttons" alternate with simple snapshots of Mommy, Daddy, and Sawyer.

Each year as the family gathers to exchange gifts, we place lighted candles in the windows. This tradition goes back to great-grandma's family. Before Jodie would open her first present this year, she had to light the candles. Great-grandma would be so happy. December 24, 2000

▲ AUSTEN AND MOMMY, Cindy Mandernach, Grand Blanc, Michigan

The mix of black-and-white and color photographs captures the timelessness of mother's love. The photos were cropped with a variety of decorative scissors.

◀ VELLUM CANDLES, Pam Klassen, Westminster, Colorado

Just as their great-grandmother always did, each Christmas holiday, this family lights candles in the windows as they gather to exchange their gifts. The layered vellum creates the perfect luminescent effect of candlelight. Vellum is also perfect for snow, stars, clouds, smoke, and sunshine.

MAKING NEW MEMORIES

Don't stop scrapbooking when they take their first steps! As your baby grows and changes—into a toddler, then a youngster, then a kid, then teenager—there will be plenty more to scrapbook about. Your child will have many new experiences and forge many new relationships, both with family and with friends. The favorite toys, the first days of school, the best pals, the Cub Scout outings—all of these are a part of your child's life story. Each deserves to be recorded and preserved on special pages of their own.

The Baby Boy who Could

AT SIX MONTHS

I want Ben's toys (especially his little cars)... I can take off my shoes and socks in about two seconds with a great big grin and have lost them everywhere (HEB, the street, etc.)... I love to ride in the front of the stroller and flirt with the ladies at the mall... I'm really cute!

AT FOUR MONTHS

I can work my way over to my "two headed bird" toy and pull it off the Gymini... I'm always losing my left sock... I have two teeth on the bottom... I love to laugh at Ben when he says "great big hug"...

NOAH'S ARK

A YEAR IN
S.S. NOAH & CO.

Noah's 2nd Year Highlights
1998-1999

Birthday Party Theme: Dragon
Soda of Choice: "Dr. Rootbeer"
Rite of Passage: Ditched the Diapers, Rides a Trike
Meanest Idea: Cutting Up Brothers Pokemon Card
Bestest Playmate: "My Friend" (pretend pal)
Game: "Who wants to play, baby bird raise their hand?"
Bad Game: Does That Hurt?
T.V.: 7:30am Zoboomafoo
Best Name Drop: "Jesus told me I sleep with You!"
Stern Quote: "You see that sign, That sign says
　　　　　NO _____!" (fill in blank with Noah's agenda)
Likely to Note Seat Belt Violations & Profanity
Song Written: "I'm working on It's My Happy Day"
Bad Habits: Blowfish Marathons & Loud Burping
Noah's Lang: Add a "kin" to the end of words
Most Sensitive to Temperature: "Coldy!"
Noah's Profanity: "You Hockey Pockey!"
Most Embarrassing Dad Moment: Pulling Down Dads
　　　Pants to Show People his "Boo Boo"
Quote to Stranger: "My Mom Pees Out of her Bottom!"
Oddest Bedtime Ritual: Kicking Himself to Sleep
Best & Worst Attribute: Easily Delighted & Offended
Best Show: Jets Taking Off After Air Show!
Goals for Next Year: Ride a Trolley, Scare My Brother,
　　　Dress Myself, Jump Into the Pool
Halloween Costume: Telletubbie
Occupational Goal: "Be a Ghost"
Favorite Sport: Anything in Water!
Best Habit: Holding Hands

▲ THE BABY BOY WHO
COULD, *(previous spread)*
JENNIFER BROOKOVER, SAN
ANTONIO, TEXAS

*Little boys love trains, and this little climber
takes Jennifer's baby boy on his first six-
month journey. Silhouetted and cropped
photos of her passenger travel in a train of
primary-colored die cuts on a track of small
brown rectangles layered on a thin black
line. The mountains are photos pieced
together and cut along their top edge. Puffy
light-blue cut clouds tell the story with letter
stickers and hand journaling.*

◀ NOAH'S ARK, SUSAN
BADGETT, NORTH HILLS,
CALIFORNIA

*A classic Bible story is the theme for these
pages featuring Noah's birthday celebration and highlights of his past year. Susan
decided to simplify her life by creating a
two-page layout for each child each
year—a very "can-do" project.*

Nicole & Isabel
Easter 1999

VELVET STAMPING

Velvet paper stamped with decorative motifs adds elegance to scrapbook pages and album covers. Be sure to work with acid-free velvet paper. You'll also need an iron warmed to a medium setting, stamps with simple motifs, and a teflon pressing cloth or paper bag.

1. Place the stamp on the ironing board, rubber side up. Cut the teflon pressing cloth or paper bag to the size of the velvet paper. This sheet will protect the velvet from the heat and imprint of the iron.

2. Place the velvet paper, right side down, onto the stamp. Be sure that the stamp is positioned so that the design motif will be exactly where you want it. Lay the pressing cloth or paper bag on top of the velvet. Press the iron onto the pressing sheet for about 30 seconds. Do not move the iron while pressing. Now, lift the sheets away from the stamp. The velvet paper will have a reverse-embossed image.

3. If you would like to add color, simply apply ink to your stamp before ironing the image onto your paper. If you choose to use velvet fabric instead of velvet paper, simply mist both sides of the velvet with water before ironing.

TIP

Be sure to include an assortment of rubber stamps in your stash of scrapbooking supplies. They are available in various sizes, shapes, and patterns—including alphabet stamps, border stamps, and theme stamps. Ink pads in a variety of colors will make stamped designs jump right off the page.

 NICOLE AND ISABEL,
ARTWORK: ERIKIA GHUMM,
BRIGHTON, COLORADO, PHOTO:
OREALYS HERNANDEZ, HOLLY
SPRINGS, NORTH CAROLINA

Muted colors and the soft elegance of velvet beg to be touched. The "reverse embossed" flowers created with simple rubber stamps and a warm iron provide the ultimate decorative touch. Just try not to run your hand across the page!

▲ LOVE AT FIRST SIGHT, TINA BURTON, MOUNDS, OKLAHOMA

Carey will be able to remember Dodger's first litter of kittens—and how he just couldn't put them down, no matter what—just by looking at this adorable page. Colorful mats and small punched circles and mini hearts frame two simply cropped photos, while the whole cut-out crew snuggling in a cheery wagon is silhouetted against a plain white background. The polka dot blanket is edged with decorative scissors and a mouse adhered to the sign enjoys the view.

◄ "I LOVE BOOKS," MISSY RICE, WHITTIER, CALIFORNIA

Missy completed these pages about her son's love of books before he was diagnosed as high-functioning autistic. "That makes the page all the more special," she says. Missy has included titles and paper illustrations of several of Zachary's favorite books, along with photographs of friends and family reading to him.

FINGERPRINT ART

Kids can add a special signature mark to scrapbook pages—their fingerprints! Select several colors of stamping ink. Stamp thumbprints and fingerprints around the edges of the scrapbook page. Press firmly and lift carefully to avoid smearing the prints. Use colored pens to transform the prints into animal figures or other designs.

▲ THUMBPRINTS, BEVERLEE BOND, GARDEN GROVE, CALIFORNIA

As her birthday gift, Beverlee's children stamped and drew these cute little creatures for her scrapbook page, starting first with their own thumbprints.

► **MICE IN THE CUPBOARDS,** CHARLA
CAMPBELL, SPRINGFIELD, MISSOURI

*The pantry was the source for props for this clever layout. Charla took
pictures of costumed children in various sitting, standing, or crawling
positions. The photos of the pantry items are sized to fit right in with
the children's antics. Silhouetted against a black background, the
photos are positioned on tan strips to represent shelves. Journaling
with a silver pen completes the page.*

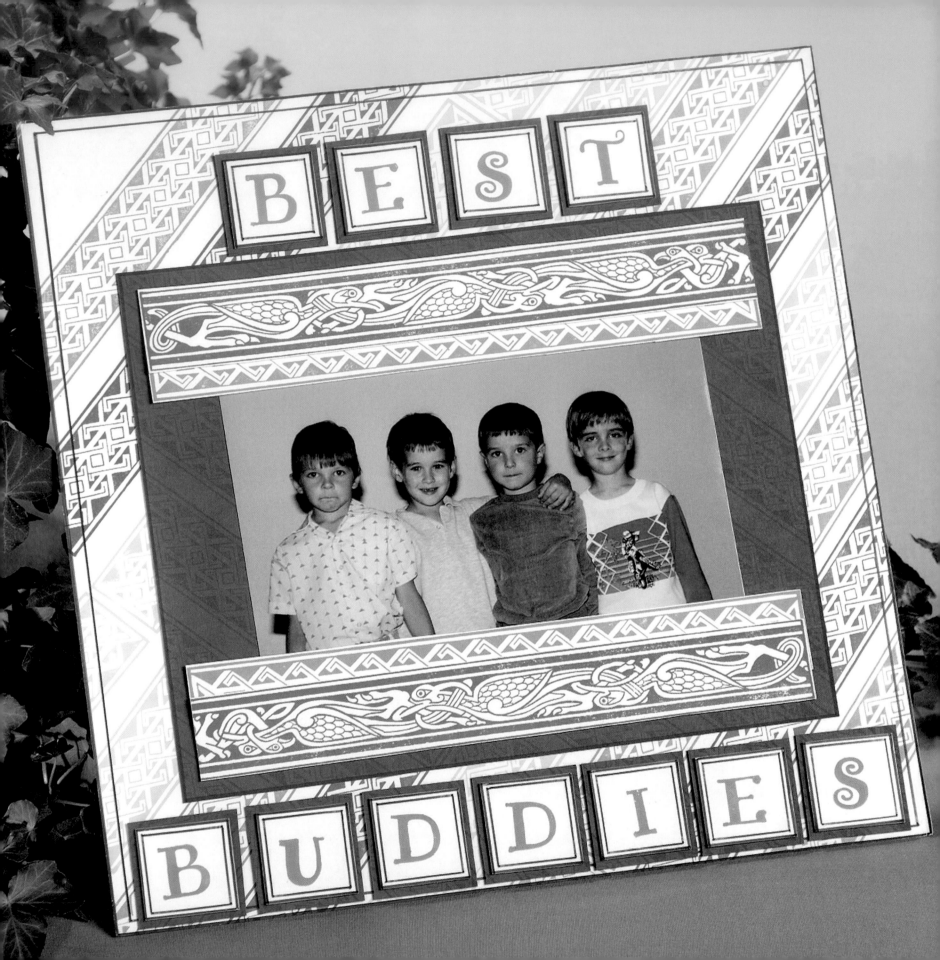

▲ LET IT SNOW, AMY ESHELMAN, INDIANAPOLIS, INDIANA

Fourteen-year-old Amy believes it is important to capture the memories of her youth. A combination of die-cut snowflakes, simple shaped, cropped, matted photos, and silhouetted photos tumble across the inventively journaled snow drifts in fun-loving profusion.

◀ BEST BUDDIES, CATHIE ALLAN, EDMONTON, ALBERTA, CANADA

Would that we could all see these fabulous "best buddies" in ten or fifteen years!

AS CHILDREN GROW

Add pages for each of your children as they grow, and, when they are old enough, encourage them to make their own pages, too. Even little kids can add their rainbow-colored handprints or crooked crayon lettering to the pages you are designing about their special achievements or favorite foods. Junior scrapbookers like fourteen-year-old Amy Eshelman became so excited about her mother's scrapbooking project that she decided to start a scrapbook of her own. Now, she and her mother attend crop parties together every Friday night, and Amy has even introduced scrapbooking to her friends.

A family's story is truly never-ending. Each generation has its own tale to tell. Your scrapbooks—and your children's and your grandchildren's scrapbooks—will link those tales together in a beautiful, imaginative, and wholly individual way.

No one can tell your family's story better than you.

TEMPLATES

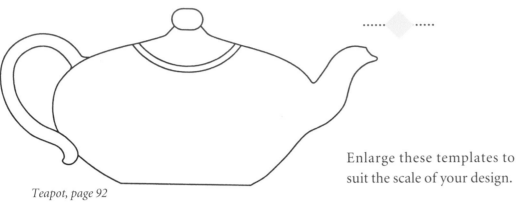

Teapot, page 92

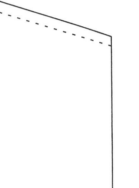

Enlarge these templates to
suit the scale of your design.

Pop-up, pages 82-83

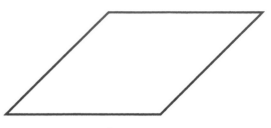

Cevron Patch, page 36

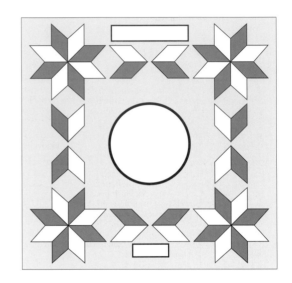

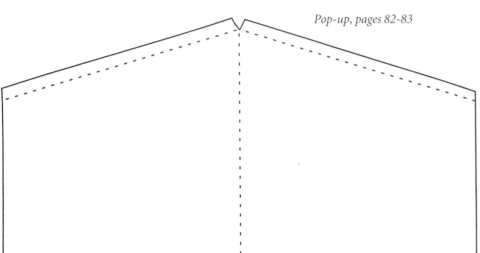

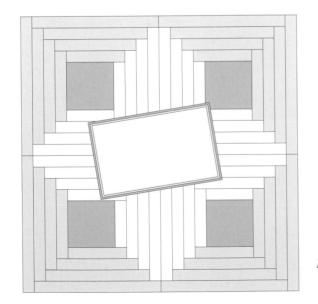

Log Cabin, pages 39

Illusion Pattern, page 69

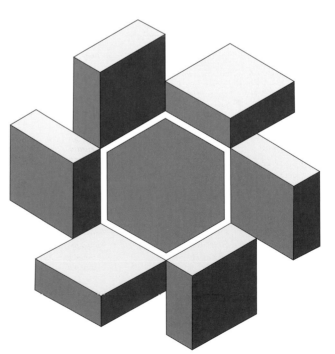

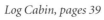

SOURCE GUIDE

Page 6 - Fourth of July
Letter stickers and number die cut - Creative Memories; other die cuts - Westrim Crafts/ Memories Forever; Number template - The C-Thru Ruler Company

Page 7 - Autumn Beauty
Diamond-shaped template - Creative Memories; Printed paper - Geographics, Inc.

Page 9 - My Grandpas
Star printed paper - The Paper Patch; Baseball paper - Provo Craft; Train, frog stickers - Sandylion Sticker Designs; All other stickers - Stickopotamus

Page 10 - My Darling Morgan
Border template - Creative Memories; Stickers - Mrs. Grossman's Paper Co.

Page 11 - My Birthday
Medium circle punch

Page 11- Rebus Disney
Template letters - American Traditional Stencils; Stickers - Mrs. Grossman's Paper Co.; Number die cut - Dayco Ltd.; All other die cuts - Ellison Craft & Design

Page 12 - They Came by Tall Ships…
Border template - Creative Memories

Page 14 - As Families Gather (Purple)
Tan floral printed paper - Making Memories; Tan spotted printed paper - Provo Craft; Letter printed paper - Hot Off The Press; Music printed paper -The Family Archives; Purple floral printed papers - K & Company; True leaf stamps made with leaves and moldable foam - Clearsnap Inc.; Leaf outline rubberstamp - Posh Impressions; Branch rubberstamp - Hot Potatoes; Leaf die cut - Dayco Ltd.; Lettering template - Delta Technical Coatings, Inc.

Page 14 - As Families Gather(Blue)
Blue vellum paper - Paper Adventures; Blue vine printed paper - Making Memories; Large blue leaf printed paper - Colorbök; Small blue leaf printed paper - MiniGraphics; Blue plaid, blue striped, blue check, and green check printed paper - Provo Craft; Blue splattered printed paper - PrintWorks; Maple leaf die cut – Ellison Craft & Design; Leaf die cut - Dayco Ltd.; Leaf outline rubberstamp - Posh Impressions; Branch rubberstamp - Hot Potatoes; Lettering template - Delta Technical Coatings, Inc.

Page 15 - Dutch Art Frames
Large and small heart, small oval, tear drop, medium tulip, mini flower and 1/8" circle punches

Page 15 - Tyler and Mom
Quilt pattern - from Baltimore Beauties and Beyond by Elly Sienkiewicz (C&T Publishing) Printed paper - Hot Off The Press

Page 16 - Generations of Family
All printed papers - The Paper Company ; Artistic wire - Artistic Wire Ltd, ; Leaf punch - Emagination Crafts Inc.

Page 17 - Passage from Russia
Brayered Ink; Frames - K & Company

Page 18 - You're Five
Floral printed paper - Current, Inc.; Other printed papers - Provo Craft; Sticker letters - Provo Craft

Page 18 - Garrett's 1st Year
Printed papers - Hot Off The Press

Page 18 - A Merry Christmas
Splatter and snowflake printed paper - Provo Craft; Dark spotted paper - Carolee's Creations

Page 20 - Kathleen Paula Kennedy
Printed paper - Hot Off The Press

Page 22 - Mom and Her Friend Cheryl
Printed vellum - Paper Adventures

Page 22 - Our Family Christmas 1997
Swirl printed vellum - Hot Off The Press; Holly printed vellum - The Paper Company; Other patterned vellum paper - Paper Adventures

Page 23 – Chili Baby
Die cut - Westrim Crafts/Memories Forever

Page 24 – My Wedding Shower
Sticker letters - Creative Memories; Circle cutter, heart punch; Umbrella die cut - Creative Memories

Page 24 - Our Family
Poem Author Unknown
Viner Hand ITC Font - Microsoft Publisher 2000 Die cut frame - Gina Bear; Punch list and instructions available through - Artful Additions

PPage 25 - Heart Quilt
Flower template - Family Treasures, Inc.

PPage 26 - The Game of Life
Letter die cut outlines - Accu-Cut

Pge 29 - Hyrum and Maria
Laser cut paper - Gina Bear; Photo corners and border stickers - Stampendous!/Mark Enterprises

Page 29 - Six Generations
Enlarged stencil - Stampendous!/Mark Enterprises

Page 30 - Family Tree
Banner template - Provo Craft; Frame stencil traced from punch shape - Family Treasures, Inc.

Page 31 - Roots and Branches
Large apple, birch and maple leaf, circle, daisy, small egg, strawberry, star, heart and mini flower punches

Page 31 - Family Tree
Leaf die cut - Handmade Scraps, Inc.; Flower stickers - PrintWorks; Title lettering style LMNOP: More Creative Lettering with Lindsay by Lindsay Ostrom (Cut-It-Up)

Page 32 - Davey Family Tree
Rhinestones - Rospack, Inc.

Page 34 - Leisure Time at the Turn of the Century
Border template - StenSource International, Inc.; Corner rubberstamp - JD Impressions

Page 35 - My Grandfather
Printed vellum - Paper Adventures

Page 36 - The Bear Family 1897
Feather-stitching stencil - StenSource International, Inc.

Page 40 – Peter Thiessen Family 1917
Printed paper - The Family Archives; Tulip punch - Carl Mfg USA; Swirl punch - Family Treasures, Inc.

Page 42 – Haying Time
Printed paper - Hot Off The Press

Page 43 - Daddy and Friends
Small and medium square punches - Family Treasures, Inc.

Page 44 - Public Sale
Leaf rubberstamp - Stampin' Up!

Page 45 - Man's Life
Printed paper - Keeping Memories Alive

Page 46 - Three Generations of Recipes
Large circle punch

Page 48 - Family Favorites
Checked printed paper - Keeping Memories Alive; Striped printed paper - Colorbök; Cherry stencil - American Traditional Stencils

Page 51 - Wedding Party
Quilling paper and supplies - Lake City Craft Co.

Page 52 - Beautiful as a Rosebud
Photo tinting supplies - The Marshall Company

Page 54 - Die Cut Window Frame
Die cut frame - Gina Bear

Page 55 - Legacy
Oriental printed paper - MiniGraphics

Page 56 - Mr. and Mrs. Anthony A. Aurelia
Border and floral stickers - Mrs. Grossman's Paper Co.

Page 57 - 50th Anniversary
Stickers - Creative Memories

Page 57 - Marriage Certificate
Corner punch - All Night Media, Inc./Plaid Enterprises, Inc.

Page 58 - Welcome Home Jim
Flag printed paper - Sonburn, Inc.

Page 58 - At Sea and on Shore
Anchor die cut - Ellison Craft & Design

Page 59 - Four Generations
Floral stickers – Creative Memories

Page 59 - Made Especially for Me
Rubberstamp – Art Impressions

Page 60 - Five Generations of Young Women
Fruit printed paper - K & Company; Purple printed paper - Making Memories

Page 64 - Piles of Smiles
Oak and Maple Punches

Page 65 - Making a Scarecrow
Leaf printed paper - Hot Off The Press; Plaid printed paper - The Paper Patch; Denim printed paper - Frances Meyer, Inc.; Scarecrow die cut - Accu-Cut

Page 65 - Holly
Quilt block stickers - Hallmark Cards; Pumpkin stickers - Melissa Neufield, Inc.

Handcoloring pens - SpotPens, Inc.; Starfish / seashell template - Delta Technical Coatings, Inc.

Page 66 - Hilton Beach
Raffia paper

Page 67 - Water Fun
Fish printed paper - "Great Papers"available at Office Depot stores

Page 68 - Thanksgiving
Tree die cut - Ellison Craft & Design; Maple leaf punch, paper crimper

Page 68 - Pumpkin Patch
Printed paper - Wubie Prints; Page topper - Cock-A-Doodle Design; Pumpkin template - Puzzle Mates

Page 69 - Pumpkin Harvest
Design pattern - by Harry Turner used with permission of Dover Publications Inc., New York; copyright 1978 by Harry Turner.

Page 70 - Snow Boarders
Tree die cut - All My Memories; Paper doll die cuts - Accu-Cut; Snowflake punches - McGill Inc. and Emagination Crafts Inc; Corner punch - Family Treasures

Page 71 - Snowy Days
Dark snowflake printed paper - Hot Off The Press; Light snowflake printed paper - Sonburn, Inc.; Snowflake sticker - Provo Craft; Star punch

Page 72 – Snow
Forest printed paper - Design Originals; Corner edgers - Fiskars; Letter die cuts - Stamping Station Inc.; Tree die cut - All My Memories' Snowflake punches - Family Treasures, McGill Inc., Emagination Crafts Inc.

Page 73 - Winter Stream
Printed paper - Creative Imaginations; Vine and snowflake die cuts - Accu-Cut

Page 73 - Blame it on El Niño
Printed paper - Sonburn, Inc.; Snowflake die cuts – Accu-Cut

Page 76 - The Dresdan Plate
Sailboat printed paper - The Paper Patch White daisy on purple printed paper - Paper Adventures; Large white daisy on green, red floral on blue, red and green floral, and pink floral without stem printed papers - Frances Meyer, Inc.; Purple vine, yellow daisy printed papers - Colors By Design; Pink floral with stem - Kangaroo & Joey; Red star printed paper - Northern Spy; Hands printed paper - Hot Off The Press; Small white daisy on green printed paper - NRN Designs

Page 79 - Our Family Traditions
Printed papers - Provo Craft, Keeping Memories Alive, The Paper Patch

Page 80 - Schoolbus Cake
Star printed paper - Paper Adventures; Sticker - SRM Press Inc.

Page 81 - Babtsia's Paska
Textured paper - Provo Craft; Corner edgers - Fiskars; Octagon template - The C-Thru Ruler Company; Corner punch - Emagination Crafts Inc.; Pink printed paper - Provo Craft; Ladybug rubberstamp - Anita Stamp available through Back Street, Inc.

Page 84 - Four Generations of Gerbrandt's
Bootie die cut - Pebbles In My Pocket; Plaid printed paper – Frances Meyer, Inc.

Page 84 - Friends and Family
Border stickers - Mrs. Grossman's Paper Co.; Printed paper - Provo Craft; Stickers - Provo Craft; Die cut frame - Canson

Page 85 - Four Generations
Printed paper - The Paper Patch; Bow template - Frances Meyer, Inc.; Heart template - Family Treasures, Inc.

Page 85 - Grandma's Gift to Amy
Printed papers - Hot Off The Press, The Paper Patch

Page 86 - Sisters in Spirit
Flowers cut from printed paper - The Paper Catalog (FLAX San Francisco)

SOURCE GUIDE COMPANY LISTINGS

Accu-Cut® (800) 288-1670
All My Memories (888) 553-1998
American Traditional™ Stencils (800) 278-3624
Art Gone Wild! (800) 945-3980
Art Impressions (800)393-2014
Artful Additions fishscraps@uswest.net
Artistic Wire Ltd.™ (630) 530-7567
Back Street, Inc. (678) 206-7373
Canson (800) 628-9283
Carl Mfg. USA, Inc. (800) 257-4771
Carolee's Creations™ (435) 563-1100
  wholesale only
Clearsnap Inc. (800) 448-4862
Close To My Heart® (888) 655-6552
Cock-A-Doodle Design, Inc. (800) 262-9727
Colorbök (800) 366-4660 wholesale only
Colors By Design (800) 832-8436
Creative Beginnings (800) 367-1739
Creative Imaginations (800) 942-6487
Creative Memories® (800) 468-9335
Current®, Inc. (800) 848-2848
Cut-It-Up™ (530) 389-2233
D. J. Inkers™ 800-325-4890
Dayco Ltd. 877-595-8160
Delta Technical Coatings, Inc. 800-423-4135
Design Originals 800-877-7820
Dover Publications 800-223-3130
Ellis on® Craft & Design 800-253-2238
Emagination Crafts Inc. 630-833-9521
Family Treasures, Inc. 800-413-2645
Fiskars, Inc. 800-950-0203
Frances Meyer, Inc.® 800-372-6237
Geographics, Inc. 404-636-5923
Gina Bear, Ltd. 888-888-4453
Hallmark Cards, Inc. 800-425-6275
Handmade Scraps, Inc. 877-915-1695
Hero Arts Rubber Stamps, Inc. 800-822-4376
Holly Craft 949-583-1426
Hot Off The Press 800-227-9595
Hot Potatoes 615-269-8002
Hygloss Products, Inc. 201-458-1700
JD Impressions 559-276-1633
Judi-Kins 310-515-1115
K & Company 816-389-4150

Kangaroo & Joey®, Inc. 800-646-8065
Keeping Memories Alive™ 800-419-4949
Lake City Craft Co. 417-725-8444
Making Memories 800-286-5263 wholesale only
Microsoft Corp. www.microsoft.com
MiniGraphics 800-442-7035
Mrs. Grossman's Paper Co. 800-457-4570
Nag Posh™ 800-333-3279
Northern Spy 530-620-7430
NRN Designs 800-421-6958 wholesale only
Paper Adventures® 800-727-0699
Papers By Catherine 713-723-3334
Pebbles In My Pocket® pebbles@pebblesin
  mypocket.com
Plaid Enterprises, Inc. 800-842-4197
Posh Impressions 800-421-7674
Pressed Petals, Inc. 800-748-4656
PrintWorks 800-854-6558 wholesale only
Provo Craft® 888-577-3545
PSX Design 800-782-6748
Puzzle Mates™ 888-595-2887
Rospak, Inc. PO Box 266 Armonk, NY 10504
Royal Stationery™ / Masterpiece® Studios
  800-447-0219
Rubber Stampede 800-423-4135
Rubber Stamps of America 800-553-5031
S.R.M. Press Inc. 800-323-9589
Sandylion Sticker Designs 800-387-4215
Sonburn, Inc. 800-527-7505
SpotPen, Inc. 505-523-8820
Stampabilities 800-888-0321
Stampendous!®/Mark Enterprises 800-869-0474
Stampin' Up! 800-782-6787
Stamping Station Inc. 801-444-3828
Stickopotamus® 888-270-4443
Susan A. Designs 978-458-6700 wholesale only
The C-Thru® Ruler Company 800-243-8419
The Crafter's Workshop 877-CRAFTER
The Family Archives™ 888-622-6556
  wholesale only
The Marshall Company Brandess-Kalt-Aetna
  Group, Inc. 800-621-5488
The Paper Catalog (FLAX San Francisco)
  888-727-3763
The Paper Company 800-426-8989
The Paper Patch® 800-397-2737 wholesale only
The Robin's Nest 435-789-5387
The Uptown Design Company 253-925-1234
Westrim Crafts/Memories Forever®
  800-727-2727
Wübie Prints 888-256-0107 wholesale only

ILLUSTRATED GLOSSARY OF TECHNIQUES

COLLAGE

Collage is a collection of different photographs or other images pasted together on a page. The elements may or may not overlapage See page 70.

JOURNALING

Journaling is just what its name implies, writing the story of your pages in words. Journaling can be as simple as a name and/or date, or it can be a full essay of the event commemorated on your page. It can also be lyrics from a favorite song, or a poem that has special meaning for you. See pages 10-13.

CROPPING

Cropping means trimming away outside edges of your photos. Cropping is used to get rid of unwanted or unnecessary parts of the photo or to make the photo fit a particular size and shape of space. See page 26.

LIFT-THE-FLAPS

Lift-the-flaps pages have windows of paper that you open to reveal a photo or journaling surprise. See page 109.

DIE-CUT FRAMES

Die-cut frames are commercially available in a variety of designs and sizes. They can be adapted to suit your own needs by additional cutting or mounting. See page 54.

MATTING

Matting is putting a frame of paper around your photo. You can place the photo onto a piece of paper that is the same shape but slightly larger than the image or make a cutout frame and placing your photograph behind it. See page 28.

EMBOSSING

Embossing involves making a paper design three-dimensional by rubbing it on a raised surface with an embossing stylus, or you can create an embossed image with embossing powder and a heat source (heat gun). See pages 115-116.

MONTAGE

Montage is similar to collage, but the pictures or parts of pictures are superimposed, or overlapped, so that they form a blended whole. See page 22.

FINGERPRINT ART

Finger- and thumbprints can be used as stamps to create a special signature scrapbook page. Decorated with colored pens the prints become handmade animal figures or other designs. See page 135.

MOSAIC

Mosaic is basically the same for the scrapbook artist as the tile artist. You cut photos into small shapes and place them on a page separated by space or a line. Photos could be cut into uniform squares and placed on a page with uniform space around each element. See page 7.

MOUNTING

Mounting simply means applying your photos or other art to your scrapbook page. See page 36.

PAPER FOLDING

Paper folding is the art of folding paper to create designs. It involves techniques similar to origami and kirigami to produce frames, borders, and embellishments for a scrapbook page. See page 20.

PAPER LAYERING

Paper layering can mean cutting out parts of a design to allow a different colored paper to show through, or placing light paper, like vellum, over an image to screen or soften the image or color underneath.. See page 112.

PAPER PIECING

Paper piecing is a technique used to construct a cut paper image from various sources—punches, free-hand shapes, or template designs. See page 114.

PAPER QUILTING

Quilt patterns lend themselves beautifully to scrap-booking pages; the logic and format make them irresistible. Quilt designs, cut from various shaped patterns, are adapted to create stunning borders, frames, or even the central motif on a large page. See page 76.

POP-UP

Pop-up is the art of cutting, folding and mounting so that when you open a two-page spread a design will "pop up" from the pages. See page 82.

PUNCH ART

Punch art uses any kind of paper punched into a shape with any of the many punches made especially for this purpose. The punched-out shapes may be used as they are or folded and combined with other shapes to create a new image. See page 74.

QUILLING

Quilling is a simple decorative technique used to embellish any kind of page. Simply roll thin strips of paper around a slotted or needle tool into various shapes and then arrange and combine the shapes to create your own design. See page 51.

SINGLE-FOLD CUTTING

Single-fold paper cutting lets you create a perfectly symmetrical design. Fold a piece of scrap paper in half, sketch one half of the design and cut it out. When you unfold the paper, you have a symmetrical template to use on your "real" paper. See page 75.

TEMPLATES

Templates are patterns used as guides in creating a drawn or cut image. See page 19.